T0149668

From Chak 29 to Dinkytown

A Memoir

FAIZ KHAN

FROM CHAK 29 TO DINKYTOWN
A MEMOIR

Holy Bible, King James Version; Regency Publishing house, Nashville, Tennessee (1978)

iUniverse books may be ordered through booksellers or by contacting:

iUniverse
1663 Liberty Drive
Bloomington, IN 47403
www.iuniverse.com
1-800-Authors (1-800-288-4677)

ISBN: 978-1-5320-6419-7 (sc)
ISBN: 978-1-5320-6420-3 (e)

Library of Congress Control Number: 2018914506

Print information available on the last page.

iUniverse rev. date: 12/26/2018

I dedicate this book to my family in Pakistan and in the U.S. who contributed so much to my happiness in life.

Faiz M. Khan

Preface

This is the story of my life – a story not only about people and events in my life but also about what I make of it right now. Upon reflection of my life, four truths become evident. First, a simple beginning is no handicap in life. Second, you make yourself what you are by making choices based on your experiences and interactions with the world. Third, life is worth living when it is self-directed. Fourth, a free mind is a beautiful mind.

Writing a memoir was not my idea. It was my wife's. She had been persistently reminding me (or should I say nagging me?) about it since I retired. My wife is American (born in Iowa) and my daughters were born in Minnesota. Although I had told my American family snippets of my life in Pakistan from time to time, my wife thought I should write the whole story before I die. She wanted me to write my autobiography for our daughters. Finally, I gave in.

Writing a book about myself seemed a little odd at first but as soon as I started I began to open up like a chatterbox. I could see myself playing, giggling, and running on the streets of the tiny village where I was born. I imagined myself living my childhood all over again. As I progressed through the manuscript, I was not only recollecting my memories of the past but also making some sense out of them. Writing a memoir is an amazing experience. It is like talking to oneself.

The book is organized into four parts. The first part has to do with my roots and early childhood. The second part is about my schooling and determination to fulfill my father's prediction of my getting the highest academic degree in the world. The third part provides a glimpse of my professional life and career as a professor and researcher. The fourth part has to do with what I call my personal enlightenment – achieving an insight into how the universe began, how life evolved on earth, and how freedom of mind is needed to reveal truths that can "set you free."

I am grateful to my wife who finally succeeded in getting me to write these memoirs. Her love is the most important part of my life.

Faiz M. Khan

Contents

Chapter 1

Where I Come From

I have been here in America for about fifty-five years and I can still get a question from someone I meet for the first time: "May I ask where you come from?" Occasionally, my answer is: "Oh, I am from Minnesota." Then the questioner clarifies: "I mean originally." I feel like saying: "There you go again!" but, surely, I don't want to be rude. So, I give the answer: "I am originally from Pakistan."

I don't think people ask these questions routinely from immigrants unless they speak with a foreign accent. I do have an accent although my dear American wife says it is hardly noticeable. My kids, who are also American, think Mom has just gotten used to it. They don't hesitate to say, even in my face, that Dad definitely has an accent. On my part, I do admit I pronounce some words a little funny and mixing them here and there in my conversation sometimes elicits laughter from my kids. Well, I take it all in good humor!

Another question I often encounter is from someone who is trying to type in my name into the computer, like: "What is your last name?" I would answer: "Khan" and then I usually follow it by spelling out K-H-A-N with a pause between each letter. Even then, what often gets put into the computer is Kahn, not Khan. Sometimes I end up saying: "It is Khan as in Genghis Khan." This invariably brings out laughter. So, it seems most Americans are more familiar with Kahn than Khan. Worse yet, many consider Khan as just a common name, like Smith or Jones. Little do they know that in the part of the world I come from, Khan is more than just a common name. It represents tribal identity – an ancestral surname.

Originally, the name Khan was used as a hereditary title by Tartar and Mongolian tribesmen of central Asia. Their leaders, Genghis Khan and his successors, used Khan as a title meaning chief or ruler. Now it is used widely as a surname in the Muslim world including Afghanistan, Pakistan, Tajikistan, and Iran.

My last name is Khan. It is my family name. It also signifies my heritage as a Pathan of Pashtun descent. The Pathan men inherit the title Khan as their surname. The Pathan women add the suffix Khanum, Khatoon, or Bibi to their names.

When I was a kid, I took delight in writing my full name with all the ancestral titles: Faiz Mohammad Khan Pathan Niazi Wada Isakhel. The word Pathan refers to the Pashtun people of Afghanistan and Pakistan. The Niazi are a subgroup of the Pashtun tribe. Niazi Pathans of Pakistan originally came from Afghanistan and most of them settled down close to the Afghanistan-Pakistan border areas such as Bannu, Isakhel, Mianwali, Bhakkar, and Balochistan. Although a large number of Niazis still live in Afghanistan, I am a descendent of the Niazis that settled in Mianwali, a district in the northwest of Punjab province of Pakistan.

Before I was born, my parents and my relatives, all Niazi Pathans, lived mostly in a village called Behu which is located in Tehsil Isakhel, an administrative subdivision of Mianwali district; hence one of my name titles is Isakhel. The title Wada, distinguished the clan of my family from those of the other Niazi groups that lived in the same area. Finally, after this long-winded explanation of my name titles, one thing becomes clear: my last name Khan is not just a common name. It has a long ancestral history behind it.

Around early 1930s, a large number of Niazi Pathans, including my family, moved to Multan, a district in the southwest of Punjab province of Pakistan (then part of India under British rule). Migration was primarily caused by the Indus River that flooded their land. My father was just a kid then and I don't know if my mother to be was born yet. My folks, relatives, and some other Niazi clans settled down in a small village, called Chak 29 (Chak in the Urdu language means village). It was surrounded by a number of other small Chaks, with their respective numbers. Most of the villagers spoke Punjabi with a Mianwali dialect, except those from one neighboring village, Chak 28, where the majority of residents spoke Pashto, the language spoken by the Pashtuns.

Besides the Niazi majority in Chak 29, there were a few minority families such as Jats and Hindus. The Jats were farmers who mostly share-cropped for a living. There were some other non-pathan families who were known by their occupation: carpenters, potters, blacksmiths, goldsmiths, weavers, water carriers (called *Mashkis*), barbers, and musicians (called *Mirasis*). The village was served by about half a dozen shops, all owned by the Hindus, that provided groceries, hardware, and other merchandise that the village needed, including buying and selling of farm goods.

My parents, who were close relatives of each other, got married when they were teenagers (probably in the range of 16 to 18 years of age). The earliest I can remember anything about my family is when I was maybe a year old or a little younger. I say that because my mother suddenly started weaning me off her breast feeding. That meant I was past the breast-feeding age (boys in that culture have to be weaned after reaching the age of one year). I remember the weaning process. It was tough but gradual. After a few days of firm but gentle rejections, I finally got the message and stopped pestering her.

My mother, who never wore a veil (called burqa) like other women in that culture, spent a lot of her time helping my father on the farm. When she was away, my sister-in-law, Bakhtawer, took care of me. She was the wife of my oldest brother, Rab. He was in the British Indian Army when I was born. He came home only when he was on leave for a month or so in a year. Bakhtawer lived with us when he was on duty with his regiment. Rab and his family stayed with us for many years, even after he retired from the army at the end of World War II. Bakhtawer raised me as her own child. She was actually like a second mother to me. Zuhra, her daughter, was younger than me by a few months; I remember her following me like a lamb.

The house where I was born (I would call it our first house because I did not know any other before then) had one bedroom and accommodated four or five small cot beds, a couple of grain bins, jars, and dishes. The family shared the walled-in compound with the cattle and about half a dozen hens, including a rooster. I remember the rooster well because he would start his crowing quite early in the morning, waking up everybody. He had a distinct crowing sound which trailed off at the end. We thought it was funny.

When I was a toddler, I remember my sister, Alam Khatoon. She was the youngest of my three sisters and was the 4th sibling, counting up from me. While my other two sisters were already married before I was born, Alam was still unmarried and lived with us. One day when I could not find her at home, I started asking for her. Someone told me that she had been married and would not be living with us anymore. I started crying and ran out of the house to find her. I still remember running back and forth on the street in a state of distress. I was so distraught that I could not utter my cry. Then somebody saw me, picked me up, and carried me to my sister's new home. There I ran up to her. She gave me a big hug and then sat down beside me to explain the situation. She told me that she would be living close by and that I could see her anytime I wanted. I suddenly realized that her new house was not very far from ours. From then on I was her frequent visitor.

I loved my first house. I remember my neighbors: one was a goldsmith family and the other made bread (called *roti*) and sweets for a living. One of the neighbor ladies operated a bread-making oven (called *tandoor*) as well as a large wok-like griddle for popping grains such as corn, wheat, and chickpeas. People could bring their own bread dough or grains. The lady would keep part of the dough or grains as her payment or accept cash. I loved popped chickpeas the best.

A traumatic incident that I can't forget happened when I was still a toddler. As a curious little boy, I frequently visited workshops of village artisans such as blacksmith, goldsmith, carpenter, potter, weaver, and so on. I was fascinated watching them at work. One ill-fated afternoon, I was at the blacksmith shop and saw a small iron wedge lying on the ground. While the blacksmith was busy with his work, I stretched my hand to grab the piece. The moment I touched it, I screamed. Apparently, the iron piece was fresh out of the burning coals and was dipped in water only once to harden it. The blacksmith attended to me immediately when he heard the scream. He dipped my hand in cold water. It didn't help much. I was still in intense pain. Though my eyes were filled with tears, I could see that the skin had sloughed off from the burnt spot.

Somebody took me home where my mother did everything to comfort me. She took me into the room and laid me on the cot. She sat by my side until I fell asleep. When I got up, I found myself alone in the room with the door closed. I tried to open the door but it was locked from the outside. I got scared. I yelled out as loud as I could for someone to open the door. I peeked through cracks in the door but didn't see anybody. I even called my neighbor's name loud but to no avail. And then I broke down and started crying at the top of my lungs; but still nothing. Finally, after crying and sobbing for a while, I fell asleep again. When I got up, the door was open and I came out. Someone ran up to me to ask how I was doing. It was explained to me that mom had locked the door when I was asleep in the room. She had to go somewhere and nobody else was home at the time. I didn't like the explanation but, well, the ordeal was over. My hand was feeling better and things went back to normal. But the incident got etched in my memory forever.

I was still a preschooler when my family moved to another house. I should mention that the house of my birth (as well as this second house) was not owned by my family. Both houses belonged to the landowners whose farms we had contracted for share-cropping. So moving to the second house meant we now worked on a different farm. At this time, four of my siblings were old enough to have moved out. But my paternal grandmother moved in to stay with us. That was great because we were very fond of each other.

My grandmother (called *Daadi* in local language) was quite old at this time. She had lost all her teeth except one. She could not eat solid food, including bread, without mashing it up first. So I would frequently mash pieces of bread and roll them up into round balls. She would eat them by chewing with bare gums. She greatly appreciated my help. Also, I would go out to the farm to hunt for baby gourds which were used as folk medicine for skin sores. She would squeeze the contents of these little round gourds on to her leg sores and then rap the area with a cloth. It must have been beneficial to her because she would often call me her precious grandson after I brought them over to her.

One morning, someone came out of the room and said Daadi had passed away. We rushed into the room. We saw her lying in her bed with eyes closed and one of her arms resting over her head. She looked like she had passed away peacefully in her sleep. Everybody started crying. Women hugged her body one by one, weeping and wailing. I was shocked. This was the first time I had experienced death in my family. I had lost my precious Daadi.

We stayed in this second house until I was about five and started my first year of school. My brother, Dost, who was next older than me and was already in 3rd grade, took me to school a few times before my father got me enrolled. Little did I know that from then on, school and education would be the most important part of my life.

Right after I became a second grader, my family bought a lot to build a house of their own. This was house #3. I was now old enough to go to school all by myself. My best playtime was at night. The street in front of our house ran north and south and intersected with a street going east and west. The intersection comprised a large square, made intentionally spacious for kids to play all sorts of games there. The ground consisted of loose dirt mixed with sand. Because of that, you didn't have to worry about getting your knees scraped. Kids of my age ran mostly barefoot (in fact I don't remember if I owned a pair of shoes then).

The playground was conveniently located close to our house – just one house away. So, I played at night with lots of kids. One memorable night, I was running on the street close to our house, barefoot as usual. All of a sudden, something hit my big toe. It felt like as if my toe had been chopped off. I screamed and went down reeling with pain on the ground, holding my toe. Kids came running to me to find out what had happened. I kept saying: something cut off my toe. Adults came to check me over. They looked at my toe but there was no sign of blood. Then somebody speculated that I could have stepped on a scorpion.

Hearing all that commotion, my mother came running out of the house to see what had happened. She sat down to look at my toe. Then she picked me up and carried me several houses away until she got to this house and called out for a person who was known in the village as a folk healer. The healer examined my toe and wrapped a cloth around my leg tightly, saying this would stop the poison from going up my leg. Thinking of it now, this probably was his version of the tourniquet procedure. Then he started chanting, in barely audible voice, probably the verses from the Qur'an. Every now and then he would stop and spit on my toe. This went on for a while but my pain did not subside. After the healer was through with his treatment, my mother carried me back home. I remember lying in bed and feeling throbbing pain in my toe for a long time. Eventually, I fell asleep. When I got up, it was early morning and the pain was completely gone. I strained my eyes to look at the toe. It was still there! I could see a tiny brown spot where the scorpion had left his mark. It may be mentioned that a dead scorpion was indeed found that morning, very close to the spot where I had gotten stung. Apparently, somebody else had seen it that night and killed it (It couldn't have been my big toe.)

During our stay in house #3, I made many friends and had no problem going out and playing with kids on the streets. I was also old enough to familiarize myself with the village streets and even go shopping on my own – usually for candy. All I had to do was take some wheat grains to the shop. The shopkeeper would weigh it, throw it into his wheat pile and give me the candy I wanted. Sometimes, if my wheat was worth more than the candy, I would get a few coins back.

I feel joy when I think about it all - my care-free childhood in Chak 29. It is always fun to reminisce about it.

Chapter 2

Grazing Water Bufflo

Once upon a time, I was a six year old boy whose off-school job was to graze our family water buffalo. As the youngest of ten brothers and sisters, my family thought it was a soft enough job that I could handle. My older brothers living with us had much harder chores to do such as cutting grass for our oxen, plowing fields, sowing crops, harvesting, etc. Our parents did share-cropping on a small farm and grew wheat, cotton, vegetables, and other crops to provide food for the family. In addition to taking care of at least one or two very young children at a time, mother worked side by side with my father. The age difference between my next older brother and me was a little more than 3 years because my mother had a miscarriage after her ninth child. The tenth child, me, probably helped her overcome her grief over that loss – I hope.

Milk was an essential commodity in a large family with kids. So, when I was growing up, we always had a good milk-producing buffalo – usually with a huge udder. I loved drinking a glass of fresh milk, right after it was milked and still warm. It was indeed a treat to have someone shoot milk into your mouth right from the buffalo's teats. Everybody laughed when the shot missed the mark, leaving you with the white stuff splattered all over your face. I don't know if the buffalo was amused by any of this but she always looked content when being milked. She liked being milked, especially when her adorable calf had the first go at it. The calf would initially suck on a flaccid teat and persistently bump its head against the udder until milk would descend and fill it. In the meantime, the mother buffalo would affectionately lick her calf's butt.

My buffalo was beautiful, considering existing standards of beauty for buffalos – medium-built, flat hairless back, small curly horns, and big shiny eyes. She also had an additional beauty mark – a distinctive white patch outlining the front of her head. Temperamentally, she was quite mellow and approachable. You could touch her face and rub your hand over her head without any sign of objection. In fact she seemed to enjoy being patted and given extra attention. She did not seem to mind if a little kid like me would take a ride on her back.

In addition to the buffalo, we had 4 or 5 oxen – bulls (also called bullocks) used for plowing fields, pulling carts, threshing wheat, and driving a rented grinding-stone flour mill, called *chakki*. Our family had a two room mud house with a walled-in compound. About half of the compound was used to accommodate the cattle, where they spent the nights, each tied to a stake. In the summer, the family members set up their bedding cots at night outside in the compound, a few feet away from the animals. If you woke up at night, you could hear the animals snorting as well as a family member or two snoring. Other than that, the stillness of night and the star-studded sky above provided unforgettable scenes. Everything seemed to be in synch with nature!

In the winter, the family slept indoors. The buffalo and her calf were quartered in the second room of the house to escape the bitterness of the cold wintry nights. The oxen were kept in a mud hut located across the street. Early in the morning, the animals were brought out of their night shelter and tied up to their assigned stakes in the compound. I still remember their foggy breath glistening in the morning sunshine. The buffalo was fed grass to get her ready for her milking session. She seemed to be in a better mood for milking while she was eating. The calf was then let loose to do her thing with her mother's udder. Someone in the family, who was known to have a magic touch for milking, would gently displace the calf off the udder and start milking. At the end, some milk was left in the udder for the calf to have a second go at it until mama buffalo would nudge the calf off with her leg.

The buffalo was milked twice a day, once in the morning and once in the evening. During the day, milk was used for drinking, *chai* (tea) and other milk by-products. Most of it went into making *makhan* (butter) and yogurt. The process (if I remember correctly) consisted of heating the raw milk to just under the boiling point and letting it cool down gradually. Then a little bit of *dahi* (curd) containing live culture was added to the milk. The mixture was left standing at room temperature (not too warm, not too cold) overnight or longer until the milk turned into dahi. In the morning, a woman family member would sit down on the floor to churn dahi with a churner stick tied to a post with a rope. She rotated the churner by pulling alternately back and forth the two ends of a rope wrapped around it. The churning continued until globules of butter would start appearing. At the end, clumps of butter were removed, leaving behind liquid called *lassi*.

As the family started waking up in the early morning, someone would light up the fire in a U-shaped mud stove, called *chulha*. One chulha was built inside a room for winter and another one outside the room for summer use. In winter, kids would be the first to gather around the stove to warm up and keep the fire going by blowing on it and adding kindling to it now and then. Pretty soon the adults would also join in as the family cook, usually my sister-in-law, or my mother, would take charge of the stove and start preparing breakfast for the family. Typically, the morning meal included items like *Chapati* (unleavened flatbread), butter, sorghum flatbread, and spinach (called *saag*), or sometime heavily buttered layered bread (called *parathas*). Parathas were everybody's favorite and my mother made the best ones. The meal was followed by tea with milk and sugar.

Women did all the housekeeping chores, including making beds, cleaning rooms and the compound, cooking meals, washing dishes, washing clothes, and hauling away animal waste from the compound to the manure heap located just outside the compound wall. They would also make patties out of buffalo dung and place them on the compound walls to dry. Dried up patties were often used as fuel to fire up the earthen stoves for cooking. All this was in keeping with the prevailing culture of a small rural village like ours. Come to think of it now, women did far more work than men. In addition to housekeeping and child care, they would also work in the fields alongside men in harvesting wheat and picking cotton. At the time, everything looked normal and natural. Family division of labor between the sexes was set by culture and not questioned or debated.

My day typically started with going to a small *Madrassa* (religious school) with one teacher and about 20 students. Here the teaching was simply about learning how to read the holy book, the Qur'an. The text was in Arabic and nobody, including the teacher, understood its meaning. What you learned here was how to read and recite the verses loud and clear. If the pronunciation did not meet teacher's approval, you could be hit by teacher's stick. Frankly, I wasn't too fond of the class because it was held very early in the morning (usually before sunrise) and also because the teacher was a tyrant. I attended the Madrassa for a year or so until I could read the Qur'an fluently.

After the Madrassa class, it was time to go to school. Our village had a small primary school for boys, grades 1- 4. It consisted of two large rooms. One of the rooms, with a bigger hall, accommodated classes for grades 1-3 and the other one was designated for the 4th grade. Depending upon the weather, the classes were held inside the rooms, in the verandas, or out in the open inside the walled-in compound of the school. There was a total of three teachers, including the headmaster. One teacher could teach and supervise up to two classes at one time.

Corporal punishment was a common practice. You could be admonished or severely punished for undesirable behavior such as not doing your homework, being rambunctious, being tardy, or giving the wrong answer to a teacher's question. The punishment ranged from striking a student on his hand with a cane; slapping him on the side of his face; or making him stand in a bottoms-up position while bringing his hands from behind the legs to touch both ears. This extremely stressful and humiliating position was to be maintained in front of the whole class for several minutes, while the teacher would continue his normal teaching routine. One of my friends, who I thought was not too bright, once told me that the standing in that crouched position was not a big deal for him because he practiced it regularly at home. I told him it was a dumb thing to do and that he should instead do his homework diligently in order to avoid the punishment. Apparently, he never took my advice because he continued to take his punishment without complaining.

Our school started around 7:00 a.m. and lasted through about 2:00 p.m., with a one hour break for lunch. Our house was not very far from the school and it was nice to just walk home for lunch. My maternal grandmother's house was even closer, not more than 50 feet away from the school compound. I often stopped there for lunch because she always had a nice treat (*mithai*) for me, such as bread pudding or crumbled bread mixed with *ghee* (clarified butter) and *gurh* (raw cane sugar). Typical lunch at home consisted of buttered bread (chapatti or *tandoori roti*) with plane lassi drink or vegetables cooked in ghee. Meat was served only occasionally, depending on if the village butcher had slaughtered a buffalo or cow that day.

After the school ended, it was time to go home and take a short nap. Afternoon tea was a favorite ritual in our family. We chatted, we laughed, and sipped chai until it was time for me to attend to my afternoon chore: to take the buffalo out for grazing. Our farm was at a walking distance, about a mile or so from the outskirts of our village. There my buffalo would be waiting for me under a tree to which she was tied with a rope. She would stand up, when she saw me coming, in anticipation of grazing. After patting her (I loved my buffalo), we would head toward the grazing grounds.

There were no grazing prairies on or near our farm. The cattle, including the buffalo, were fed cut grass that we grew on our farm. But the buffalo got an extra treat. I would take her to the fields for grazing. She was allowed to graze only on the spots where the grass had been cut. She did a thorough job of mowing down the grass remnants close to the ground. I kept a close watch on her so that she would not extend her grazing range to the uncut parts of the field or, worse, stray into nearby fields of sugar cane, wheat, or cotton.

The best grazing spots for my buffalo, however, were the banks of irrigation channels that crisscrossed our farm and the communal irrigation streams that had been dug and maintained collectively by the villagers. The villagers took turns to divert water from the streams to the channels on their respective farms to water their fields. Even if the farm channels were dry most of the time, grass would grow on their edges. In the communal streams, however, the water flowed year around and plenty of grass could be found along their banks. So, I had the option of letting my buffalo graze on the farm channels or the nearby streams, depending on which ones had the most abundant grass at a given time of the year.

After the grazing session was over, I would bring the buffalo back to her usual abode under the tree. There she and I would rest in the shade until one of my brothers, Satar, working nearby in the fields, would stop by to ensure that the buffalo had been fully fed. With the buffalo standing, he would check depressions on both sides of her belly. If the depressions did not look full, that would mean that the buffalo's tummy was not full. In that case, she would need more grazing. Because I did not want to flunk this inspection, I would often wish that the buffalo would not defecate before inspection. It was just wishful thinking!

Although I loved my buffalo, the daily chore of grazing her was not all fun. It was a boring job but it was an assigned chore that I was responsible for doing. In fact, what I missed most was having some playtime with my friends in the afternoon instead of tending to a grazing buffalo for hours. Every time I moaned and groaned about it in front of Satar, he would smirk and say that I had all kinds of playtime at night. Satar was like a foreman when it came to doing farm chores. So there was no point arguing with him about the grazing issue.

In spite of the tedium of daily grazing, there was one thing that I didn't mind at all doing. I liked riding on my buffalo's back while she was grazing. When I took her to a stream, she would typically first drink water and then find a wider spot to plop herself down to wallow in the water. She would immerse her whole body in the water except her nostrils. After wallowing to her heart's content, she would finally stand up and start grazing on vegetation growing on the banks. While she was busy grazing, I would look for a spot with a high enough bank from where to hop on her back. She didn't mind, probably because I was a real light weight at that age.

Riding on the buffalo's back for an hour or so was a bit tedious for me (but definitely not for the buffalo). Often times I would lie down on her back to rest. I would try not to fall asleep but sometimes I just couldn't help. I remember falling off while asleep one time. The incident happened when I slipped off her back and fell into the stream. That was not only a rude awakening, I found myself on top of a thorny bush immersed in the water. I uttered a big ouch. When I extricated myself from the bush, I found a number of thorns stuck in my back. I felt severe pain. I stretched my arm to reach the spot on my back. It was bleeding. I was able to pull out all the thorns except one that was stuck in far back and out of my hand's reach. I got the buffalo out of the stream and headed straight home. Everyone tried to comfort me. I wasn't crying but they could see that I was in lot of discomfort. The pain didn't stop until someone was able to pull the last thorn out. The ordeal was finally over!

After the above episode, I got convinced that going to sleep while riding a buffalo is not a good idea. Another event had an even more everlasting impression on me. It occurred when I was a bit younger. One afternoon, I was grazing my buffalo in a stream that ran adjacent to our farm. This part of the stream happened to have high banks. I was on my buffalo's back as usual while she was grazing. All of a sudden there was a sudden sound and the buffalo got spooked. She climbed out of the stream with great effort and started running as fast as she could. I held on to her for a few seconds and then got thrown off her back. The next thing I remember is laying on the ground and one of my brothers standing over me to help. I also noticed that my buffalo was sitting by my side. Later my brother told me that when he heard the commotion, he came running to the spot where I had fallen. I was laying on the ground unconscious and the buffalo sitting beside me. Miraculously, I did not receive any serious injury – just a few bruises.

When we came home, everyone was touched by the story. I have reflected many times over the years as to what must have prompted my buffalo to sit down by my side after I fell. Whatever the answer, it is refreshing to know that animals also have a heart!

Chapter 3

Dusty Streets of Chak 29

My family built a new house by the time I got to be a third grader. It was our fourth house and it turned out be our last one in Chak 29. This time the house had several improvements: 5 spacious rooms, a *baithak* (parlor) for guests, and two airy shade structures to provide shelter from the sun and hot weather in the summer. The house was constructed out of mud bricks, formed by local brick makers – it was always fun for me to watch them mold the bricks from mud into perfect shapes. A wooden gate at the entrance of the house provided a distinctive look. It was an antique door with an iron ring on the outside; presumably used originally to tie up horses. We had no horses but I had fun playing with the ring.

The new house was located on the outskirts of the village and a couple of houses away from my school. The location was ideal also because it abutted a natural wilderness area, with bushes scattered here and there and a number of tall sand dunes that were sculpted anew every time the wind blew. The sand dunes were a great place for kids to play all sorts of games such as climbing up the dune tops and sliding down. Another popular game was to drop round objects from the top to see how far they would roll down. You could win a few rolling pebbles if yours rolled down the farthest. In the summer, though, you could not play on sand except in the cool mornings or evenings. The sand got too hot at mid-day to walk on with bare feet.

The hub of village activity was the village square, located at the center of the village. In the middle of the square, there was a communal well that was the main source of water supply for the whole village. It was a deep well and kids, including myself, often peeked into it to look at the pool of water at its bottom. The water from the well was drawn out by a water wheel, consisting of a chain of buckets hung around a vertical wooden wheel turned by a system of interlocking cogs. It was powered by an ox (a bullock or a male water buffalo) yoked to a long wooden beam that moved the wheel in a circle. Water-filled buckets would empty into a trough that channeled the water into a big square water reservoir. The reservoir was built on ground with bricks and cement and had a removable top for cleaning. It was fitted with water spigots all around it so that several people could draw water from the reservoir at the same time.

Surrounding the village square were about half a dozen shops, the village mosque, and a few residential homes. There was plenty of open space in the square for people to do shopping, get their water from the well, have social gatherings, and so on. It was also a good place for vendors to sell their merchandise, set up make-shift stoves for making sweets such as *laddus*, *jalebis*, *kabobs*, and other popular food items.

The village square was also a good place for kids to play. If you got thirsty, the water was readily available from the spigots close by. Because of frequent water puddles left around the water reservoir, it was a favorite place for bees and wasps to hang around. Most kids were afraid of them but some, including me, actually liked to play with them. For example, I would slowly bring my hand close to a sitting wasp and then swiftly grab its head while keeping my fingers away from its stinger. Then, I would carefully pull the stinger out by pressing its tail with a stick. After this delicate operation, the wasp was rendered harmless. I would tie a long thread to one of its legs and tie the other end of the thread to a post. The wasp was then let go. You could watch it fly round and round, like a helicopter. I must admit, thinking of it now makes me feel guilty. It was not a humane thing to do to a poor living thing.

The well was crowded in the mornings and late afternoons. You could see lots of people, mostly women, getting their earthen pitchers (*ghara*) filled with water from the spigots. You could see a steady stream of women in the streets carrying pitchers on their heads. Every now and then, you could see a *mashki* (water carrier) carrying his water-filled goat skin bag (*mashak*) on his back. Many families, including ours, relied on Mashkis to deliver well water to their homes on a daily business.

Just before sunset, you could see farmers bringing their cattle home and raising clouds of dust in the streets. Once in a while, you could see a shepherd herding his sheep and goats. All this animal and people traffic every day pulverized the streets into fine dust – a mix of sand, dirt, and animal waste. To us kids, the dusty streets of Chak 29 were nothing but a perfect playground with soft and cushy turf on which to run, play, and wrestle.

Dozens of boys would gather at night to play games. There were no street lights (the village had no electricity) but with the clear star-studded skies above, who needed them? Sometimes if there were enough kids, we would split into two teams and play our version of American football (but without a football). The team on the offense would have one running back, protected by its offensive tackles. The opposing team on defense would attempt to catch the runner while trying to avoid being blocked by the opposing tackles. The runner had to get to the goal post (a land mark like a tree or street intersection) without being caught by the defensive players. My specialty was being the running back.

Another night game was hide-and-seek. Again, there would be two teams, one choosing to hide and the other to seek. The game was played in some well-defined hiding areas outside the village boundaries. The game could last way into midnight. I don't know if there were any parental curfews in vogue then, but my father had instructions for me to be home well before midnight. If I cheated, I had the good fortune of having an alibi witness – usually my niece Zuhra – who would vouch for me if someone had told on me for being late.

Night games were mostly fun and the families didn't mind noisy kids running around in the streets late at night. Overall, the kids were well-behaved except for one night that I remember even to this day. It was close to midnight and almost time for us to split and go home. We happened to be just outside a house that was known to have a watermelon patch inside their compound. Someone suggested that it would be nice to snitch some melons. We saw a small opening in the compound wall, just wide enough for one person to get through at a time. The opening was closed shut by a wooden door. One of the kids was strong enough to push the door open and a couple of kids got inside. They would pick the melons and pass them on to us through the door opening. After gathering a few melons, the snitching operation stopped. We took the melons to a nearby stream and had a great party!

Thinking of it now, our village life was quite gregarious. We enjoyed kids games as well as adult sports. Wrestling and *kabaddi* (a team sport played in Punjab), were the most popular sports in our area. These were inter-village sport events held at a preselected venue every year with great fanfare. Village musicians (called *Mirasi*) were hired to entertain the fans with double headed drums (called *dhol*) and reed instruments (called *sharnai*). I enjoyed these events immensely because one of my brothers, Haq Nawaz, was a well-known wrestler and kabaddi player. Two other brothers, Shah Nawaz and Zulfiqar, who were then in the British Indian Army and Air force, respectively, were track and field runners. My family, in general, was very much sports minded, probably because my father who had been a wrestler and weight lifter in his younger days, was an avid fan of sports.

As a kid growing up in a small rural village, I have wonderful memories of a carefree but down to earth life full of fun and play. There were occasions that offered plenty of entertainment for kids and adults alike. Weddings were celebrated with great pomp and show; the village rocked with music at these events. Also, wandering musicians with a variety of instruments such as drums, *tablas* (pair of small drums), harmoniums, and bagpipes, would occasionally stop by to entertain the music fans, who would put down some money in the musicians' bowl at the end of each performance.

Our village also attracted snake charmers. Everyone was mesmerized by watching a cobra with its expanded hood dance to the *bean* music. Bean is an instrument made from a hollow gourd, has two reed pipes and a mouth-blown air chamber. A couple of times, I saw a snake charmer play snake detective. He would walk around a house and then declare that a snake had been sighted there. The homeowner had no choice but to ask him to catch the snake. The cost was negotiated and the snake charmer would start the search by playing particular notes on his bean to coax the snake out. After searching several nooks and corners, lo and behold, the snake would appear, resulting in a big sigh of relief on homeowner's part. The incident was talked about for several days; some believing that the drama was real while others asserting that the snake was not wild but a well-trained snake charmer's pet.

Besides the fun games, sports, and music, a number of festivals were celebrated annually in our village. Among these, *Eid-ul-Fitr* was the most popular. This is a religious (Islamic) holiday, marking the end of the fasting month of Ramadan. The night before Eid, kids would coat their hands with an herbal dye called *henna* (we called it *mehndi*). First thing in the morning, the dried-out henna was washed off the hands to reveal the red-colored skin beneath. You could hear the kids screaming with joy and showing off their dyed hands to the adults. The luckiest one with the reddest hands would be declared the winner!

On Eid day, it was a custom for kids to wear new clothes while adults adorned themselves in their best costumes. All adults would first go to the mosque and offer Eid prayers, led by an *Imam* (religious leader), before starting the day of celebration. Women would begin their day by making a variety of sweets for the family. Typical sweet dishes in our family were cooked noodles with milk and raw cane sugar (*gurh*), and *suji halva*, a confection made with semolina flour (coarsely ground endosperm of wheat) and a variety of other ingredients to enhance flavor and taste.

The second Eid, called *Eid ul-adha*, commemorating the Prophet Abraham's willingness to sacrifice his son at God's command, was celebrated by sacrificing an animal for meat. Adults would often share the cost of a sheep, goat, or a cow for slaughter. The meat would then be distributed among relatives, neighbors, and the poor. One third of the meat was kept for the family. Normally, most families, including ours, consumed meat only sparingly. But the meat was abundant on this day and several days afterwards as the leftover meat was salted and dried for future use.

In contrast to the happy festivals, we observed ten days of mourning every year in memory of Imam Hussein, the grandson of the Prophet Muhammad. Imam Hussein and most of his followers (including his family members, children, and adults) were massacred in a place called Karbala, in present day Iraq, by the army of Yazid ibn Muawiya, the second caliph of Umayyad caliphate. The battle of Karbala happened on the tenth day of Muharram, in the year of 61 AH of the Islamic Calendar (Oct. 10, 680 CE). This was undoubtedly the greatest tragedy in the history of Islam and had the greatest impact on the religious conscience of Muslims.

On the day of Ashura (Muharram 10th), we commemorated the death of Imam Hussein with sorrow and tears. Even to this day, I cannot comprehend the abhorrence of the act of those who called themselves Muslims and yet cold-bloodedly murdered the family of the Prophet – the Prophet they believed in as the Messenger of God. Again, when I watch terrorists of the modern era, who also call themselves Muslims, perpetuate atrocities on innocent people, Muslims and non-Muslims alike, I cannot help getting the sick feeling that things have not changed much since the brutal murder of Imam Hussein and his family.

As a silver lining to my faith in humanity, I should mention that in our village we also participated in the Hindu festivals of *Holi* and *Diwali*. These festivals were celebrated every year by Hindu families in our village but Muslims would also join in. Holi was children's favorite because it involved spraying bright colors on each other while laughing, playing, and dancing.

At the time I was growing up in Chak 29, Hindus and Muslims lived like one big human family. But, alas, this religious harmony and tolerance would soon be shattered. A year after I finished my 4th grade, the Indian sub-continent was on the verge of being partitioned into Hindu-majority India and Muslim-majority Pakistan. In the next few years, there would be a bloody civil war in India between Hindus and Sikhs on one side and Muslims on the other. Close to 15 million people were displaced along religious lines and more than a million perished. Man's inhumanity to man lay bare in every nook and corner of the new India and Pakistan.

Lots have been written and analyzed regarding the partition. Now, after 71 years, who is to blame for the murderous rampage that ensued? Was it the British government and its faulty partition plan? Was it the politics of Hindu and Muslim nationalist parties at the time that were hell-bent on partitioning India along religious lines? Would it have been better to have a united India after the British left? We could go on and on debating these issues but one must realize that it is hard to objectively evaluate alternative courses of actions after the event has already taken place. It is like playing "Monday morning quarterback," as they say in America.

Chapter 4

Road to the Top of the Class

It may sound a bit nerdy, but from the very start I loved going to school. Not only was I excited to learn new things at school, it was a great place to socialize. The constant chatter of kids felt like music to my ears, especially when I contributed to it. Singing nursery rhymes to learn alphabets and numbers was fun!

The only thing I did not like about school was the teacher's harsh discipline. Watching corporal punishment being dished out to little kids was especially hard to watch. But I soon learned that the best way to avoid teacher's wrath was to do well in the class. Accordingly, I studied hard, did my homework diligently, and did everything in my power to avoid punishment. More importantly, I found out that being smart not only earned you the respect of teachers but also of your peers. Whatever the underlying reason, I felt inherently motivated to excel in school. I did not succeed all the time, but the competitive drive I cultivated early on stayed with me throughout my life.

As I progressed from grade one through three, I realized that I had developed a special affinity for math. While most kids in my class hated math, I loved it. I would practice math for hours at home so that I could do well in the tests at school. I was okay in reading and writing, but math was my specialty. Consequently, I started to gain the reputation of being smart not only in my class but also in my village. When people would call me smart into my face, it made me feel a little awkward on the outside but happy on the inside. By the time I reached the third grade, I was officially made the classroom monitor. Finally, I had reached my goal of being at the top of my class!

I stayed at the top of my class until I finished my fourth grade. During this time, I was liked by my teachers and got along wonderfully with my classmates. My family was proud of me. Although my parents never went to school, they praised me every time I scored the highest in my tests. Three of my older brothers, Shah, Z.A., and Dost had also the reputation of being bright in school, but my father often said that I was destined to get the highest degree in education. He was my biggest cheer leader.

Throughout my fourth grade studies, I had been preparing hard for the final exam which was conducted district-wise to competitively award merit scholarships. The exam was held in a small town about two to three miles away from our village. I remember that day sitting on a playground among hundreds of students from surrounding villages and nervously waiting for the exam to start. When it finally did, the first question was a math problem. It didn't take me long to solve it. I was the first one to put down my slate and raise my hand, meaning that I was done with it. After everybody was finished, the exam supervisor came and marked each slate with a notation of correct or incorrect answer. When I looked at my slate, I could not believe my eyes. My solution was marked incorrect. I soon realized that I had missed a carryover number in the problem involving addition. I had not taken the time to double-check my arithmetic. With that error on my mind, I struggled through rest of the exam.

After the exam was over, I developed a headache. On my way home, I briefly sat down to eat my snack. A few minutes later, I threw up. Although I felt a little bit better after throwing up, I still couldn't get over my sick feeling about the exam. When I got home, I was greeted by my family with questions like how did the exam go. While I was telling them about my error, I broke down. They all comforted me and tried to cheer me up. But it took a long time for me to settle down and get over the sick feeling.

The next day, my teacher reported that I had passed the exam but my performance did not merit the scholarship. I was devastated. It took me a while to accept the outcome and move on. Now it was time to think about the fifth grade. How could I get to be the top of the class again? Learning from my past experience and my performance in the fourth grade exam, I made a firm resolution that I would study harder than ever and that I would always double-check my answers in the exams. I stuck to that resolution throughout my future schooling.

For my fifth through tenth grade education, I had to move to a different school. I got admission to D. B. High School, Kacha Khuh, where my brother Dost was already a seventh grade student. Dost and I stayed in a rented house with a couple of other students from Chak 29. The house was located close to the school grounds where we spent most of our afternoons playing soccer and other sports.

Kacha Khuh is a good size village in the district of Khanewal. It is linked with the major cities of Lahore and Multan by a railroad and a national highway, both passing through the middle of it. The school is located on one side of the railroad and a major highway on the other, both less than a kilometer from each other. A bazaar, known as Raja Bazaar, runs along both sides of the highway. It includes rows of shops with attached houses in the back and a few restaurants and hotels. About a kilometer away from the bazaar is an irrigation canal, one of many that originate from the river Sutlej as it runs its course through the Punjab.

Coming from Chak 29, Kacha Khuh was like a big city to me. I liked the red-brick school with large class rooms, ceiling fans, student desks, chairs, and blackboards. Classes were quite structured, followed a set time schedule, and the school bell chimed at the end of each class. Students were mostly drawn from Kacha Khuh and neighboring villages. There was plenty of ethnic diversity that included Pathans, Jats, Hindus and Sikhs. This was the time just before India was partitioned.

The front yard of the school was split into two areas by a pathway leading to the school building. On one side was an open space where students would gather for the morning drill and roll call. The other side was a landscaped garden of colorful flowers. Across the street from the school building was a small hospital (we called it dispensary). It had a large flower garden in front of it. I loved to walk through the garden every now and then. Although plucking flowers was not allowed, it did not deter me from plucking some big roses and fragrant jasmine flowers (when nobody was looking).

In spite of new students and a different school environment, I felt at ease in the class. I studied hard as I had promised myself after that fourth grade exam experience. I began to regain my old confidence. I felt bold enough to often raise my hand voluntarily to answer teachers' questions. Socially, I got along well with fellow students. I made a number of new friends, both at school and in the town.

I spent summer vacations at home in Chak 29. I was so motivated to excel in the class that I had planned to use summer vacations to prepare for the final exam ahead of time. But soon bad things began to happen all over India. News of massacres and atrocities started trickling in from neighboring towns and villages. The dreaded partition of India had begun. I was eight years old then. I remember my family waking up at night to the sound of gunfire. Adults would arm themselves with knives, spears, and whatever weapons they could get their hands on. We had one shot gun which one of my brothers would get ready and keep loaded. Fortunately, all these warnings of attack on our village turned out to be false alarms.

In a week or two, all Hindu families living in Chak 29 had left without an incident. But the news from some other towns and villages was not as good. There was one report that especially shocked my family and me. We learned that a teacher in my Kacha Khuh school had kidnapped our Headmaster's two daughters (they were Hindus). We later learned that the sisters were being held in a house in Chak 29. While it was still a rumor, we saw one day soldiers surrounding the house we had suspected. The soldiers were from the British Indian Army and were armed with rifles and machine guns. Being a kid, I had no fear of approaching one of the soldiers and closely looking at the hardware he was wearing. Fortunately, the kidnapped sisters were rescued and led to the army jeep waiting for them. Thinking of that incident now, my heart goes out to the two sisters. I hope they were reunited with their family.

Partition of British India created two independent countries, India and Pakistan, on August 14 – 15, 1947. The Punjab province got split into two parts: Muslim majority areas in the West, where we lived, became part of Pakistan while the Hindu and Sikh majority areas in the East became part of India. Although, people could legally stay in either of the newly created countries, most Muslims in India decided to move to Pakistan and most Hindus and Sikhs in Pakistan moved to India. The partition of India displaced over 10 million people along religious lines. A large-scale violence broke out everywhere and one to two million lost their lives. The enormity of this calamity is simply mindboggling.

When I went back to school in Kacha Khuh after the summer vacations, I couldn't believe my eyes. All the Hindu and Sikh students, including my close friends had left. You could feel the sadness all over. It took quite a while before the school started functioning normally. For many years, I entertained the hope that someday I would meet my Hindu and Sikh friends. But it never happened. Only the memories remain!

In the aftermath of the partition, many shops operated by Hindus and Sikhs in Kacha Khuh became vacated. My family, who had wanted to move to Kacha Khuh for quite some time, found the opportunity to rent one of the shops. My oldest brother, Rab, who was now a retired Sergeant Major in the Indian army, set up the shop as a general store that included merchandise such as hardware, farm equipment, household items, and buying and selling of locally grown wheat and cotton.

Attached to the back of our shop was a small two bedroom house with a walled-in compound. Rab's wife, Bakhtawer, moved in to manage the household as well as take care of Rab, Zuhra, Dost, and me. In fact, my family now had two houses, one in Chak 29 and one here in Kacha Khuh. My parents and my brother Haq's family still lived in Chak 29.

I liked to spend my weekends and holidays in Chak 29. I would pack up my books in a bag (called satchel) and walk about six miles to commute between Kacha Khuh and Chak 29. In order to overcome the boredom of this walk, I would often daydream. The most common one of these daydreams involved a tiny car, with no top. I would be driving the dream car en route to Chak 29 waving to my friends as they passed by me.

By the time I got to be a sixth grader, I was well-entrenched in the school and town life of Kacha Khuh. To be at the top of the class was still my goal. A couple of students gave me a good competition but that motivated me all the more to achieve my goal. When the final exam arrived, I was well prepared. I beat my competition and was declared first in my class. Not only that, I was named the class monitor. I retained that position until the tenth grade, the final year of my high school.

Being the class monitor provided great experience for me. I assisted the teacher in teaching, which in turn helped me understand the subject matter better. After all, you can't teach it to others unless you understand it yourself.

Chapter 5

Making Home in Kacha Khuh

In the early days of my childhood, we lived on whatever cash crops we grew on our farm. That was barely enough for my parents to raise a family of ten kids. But as the kids grew up, things got a little bit better as two of my brothers (Shah and Z.A.) finished their high school and enlisted in the army. Together with my oldest brother Rab, who was already in the army, the three of them would send some money home to help us. I was the youngest of the family and I never thought of whether we were rich or poor. I loved my family as it was and I would not trade it with anybody for a better one.

When we started a business in Kacha Khuh, it was a turning point for my family's finances. We rented a shop in the Raja Bazaar that turned out to be a good venture. After a year or two, the family started weaning off from farming. Soon my older sisters and their families, as well as some of my relatives, moved to Kacha Khuh and started their own businesses. Many of them kept their Chak 29 connection by keeping their houses and/or their farms there. My family eventually gave up farming altogether but kept the house "with the big gate" as a second home for many years to come.

After giving up farming, my brother Satar, who was four or five years older than me, joined Rab to run the shop. As the business got better, Satar opened another shop in partnership with my nephew, Qadir (the eldest son of my sister, Sardar). Satar mentored Qadir in running the shop and they expanded the merchandise to include textile, hardware, and straw materials commonly used by the local population. Pretty soon, the shop was doing extremely well. Eventually, Satar and Qadir split the business and Qadir took over the second shop.

Satar happened to have a keen business sense. He would travel to big cities like Lahore and Multan, negotiate discounted prices for the goods and buy them on credit. He would then sell them in his shop with a reasonable profit margin. On his return visit to the city stores, he would pay off the debt and buy more goods on credit. Using this method, he was able to build some capital, enough to start yet another shop. This was a small shop, called *Khokha*, to sell handicraft, household items, and farm implements. I would sometimes help Satar to run the Khokha shop when I was off school. With the price book in hand, I had learned how to make a good sale pitch and even how to deal with a haggling customer.

While I was still a high school student, Shah got married to the daughter of our close relative, Iskander Khan. This was arranged to be a camelback wedding. The bride and the bride's maids rode the well-decorated lead camel, followed by a caravan of camels carrying women and children. The groom rode a horse and the rest of the men in the wedding party had their own transportation. Because I was the bridegroom's kid brother, I rode the camel with the bride. This was my first and the only ride on a camel's back. I felt a little bit air-sick but who would complain of such a lofty ride?

The wedding procession started from Kacha Khuh and ended by our house in Chak 29. Soon the guests were entertained in a carpeted tent with food, dancing and music. The guests then came out of the tent and sat outside, forming a big circle. In the middle were musicians playing drums, *shehnai*, and other popular instruments. Every now and then, a guest would wave money to the musicians. The lead musician would approach the guest, take the money and singingly announce the name of the guest as well as the amount of money. This money was intended as gift for the groom. After the music program was over and all the gift money collected, the musicians would get a certain percentage as a tip, in addition to the contracted price for their services.

Because my family's move to Kacha Khuh coincided with the aftermath of India's partition, I witnessed firsthand how the mass migration of refugees looked. It is heart wrenching. As a kid, I could not fully apprehend the events behind this colossal tragedy, but I do remember the harrowing scenes. Trains of bullock carts, loaded with household goods, women, and children, moved day and night on the highway through Kacha Khuh. It wasn't infrequent to see men carrying the old and decrepit on their backs. Those walking on foot looked exhausted. We did not know where in India they had started their journey or where in Pakistan they were going. But they were all headed west. Our teachers had instructed us to carry water to the refugees when we saw them passing through the town. We all did whatever we could to alleviate their suffering.

The violent nature of the partition sowed seeds of hostility between India and Pakistan, which persists even to this day. The two countries have fought several wars over the disputed territory of Kashmir. Currently, they are both nuclear powers, and, as a result, cannot afford to initiate a major conflict. But an atmosphere of resentment over the partition continues to plague their relationship. Good people on both sides acknowledge that this long-held animosity is detrimental to the interest of both countries. But little real progress has been made to heal the wounds of partition.

After the turmoil of partition was over, things settled down and normalcy returned. My daily life mostly revolved around school, business, family, and friends. Of these, the school got most of my attention. I loved competition to excel. I prepared for exams like athletes prepare for the Olympics. For example, I had a classmate named James who was known to be very bright. We often studied together after school. Secretly, I took it upon myself to beat him in one of the exams (I think it was the seventh grade final exam). After studying together on the day before the exam, he forgot to take his textbook home. When I realized that without the textbook he won't be prepared for the exam, I took the book to his home. I thought that the competition must be fair and square!

Besides studies, I loved sports. Track and field games were my passion. My specialty was the 100 meter dash. I learned to emulate Jesse Owens (American athlete) style of running from the pictures I had seen in a sports magazine. I also liked to play soccer but wasn't as competitive. The same went for the long jump, high jump, volley ball, and badminton. One year, our school participated in a district-wise soccer tournament. Our team, of which I was a member, got badly beaten. It was a complete shutout. After that, I played soccer for enjoyment only.

In the summer, the days would sometimes get unbearably hot. People would gather on the banks of the nearby irrigation canal to cool off. That is where I learned my swimming. The water looked brown (presumably from the river silt) but no one cared. It was for bathing and swimming, not for drinking. The canal was also a good spot for kids to show off their diving and swimming skills. On a calm day, skipping stones was a favorite sport.

During summer nights, people slept outside in the open. Men and boys would set up their cots (called *charpoys*) and beds in front of their shops. Before saying good night, I liked to join in the stories and gossips of the day. That was also the time for the comedians among us to try their jokes. In our family, Shah was the biggest jokester. His down to earth jokes would put you in stitches. Thinking about them now can still make me laugh. Those were the great times of my life!

One of my favorite pastimes was to go to the railroad station and watch the trains pass by and stop. Along with other kids, I also did some dumb things like walking on tracks, putting a penny (*paisa*) on the track and letting the train pass over it, and walking across the gap between two railroad cars of a stationary freight train. The latter was a common practice among kids as well as adults because these super-long trains would block direct access between the school and the bazaar for hours. The only gated road access across the railroad tracks was about a kilometer away, used mostly by busses and other vehicular traffic.

The railroad station was also a source of business for an entrepreneur like Satar. He invested in renting out cots to passengers who got off the train at night or had to catch a late night train. He would set up these cots in an open area outside the railway station as well as some inside a railway building, built for passengers (called *musafirkhana*). Satar and my nephew Qadir would stand at night near the railway station, approaching passengers and hawking their cots for rent. I didn't mind sometimes assisting them in this endeavor. After the cot renting was done, I would setup a bed for myself on one of those cots and sleep the whole night. We all thought it was such a lucrative business!

Since it had a high school, hospital, railway station, national highway, bazaar, and a swimmable canal, Kacha Khuh offered a lot more amenities than Chak 29. Adding to these amenities, I got my first bicycle. It was an adult bike, to be shared with my brothers. But I practically hogged it. Although my feet didn't reach both paddles at once, I loved biking around, paddling with one foot at a time. Most importantly, I could now bike to Chak 29 on weekends without having to walk on foot for six miles. Things got even better when my both feet could reach the paddles. I think that happened when I reached the ninth grade.

During the tenth grade (the final year in high school), I was more focused on studying for the final exam (called matriculation exam). This exam was offered at one time for all schools in the University of Punjab. You had to pass this exam to become eligible for a college admission. And if the score was high enough, you could merit a scholarship for two years in college. The site of examination for our school was in a town called Mian Channu, about 14 miles from Kacha Khuh. The exam took a few days to cover all subjects. At the end, I thought I had done well but wasn't sure if I would merit a scholarship.

I had to wait a month or two before the results were published nationally in the newspaper. I passed the exam. I ranked first in my class but nationally, I wasn't sure if my standing was high enough to merit a scholarship. All along, I had dreamed about the scholarship. But now its chances looked kinda iffy.

My determination to go to college was well known to my family but the question always came up about the finances. My father had made clear his intentions by often saying that I was destined to get the highest degree in education. My mother came up with a solution: she volunteered to go with me and take care of the cooking and cleaning while I attended the college. My brothers agreed to help as well. So, I got the green light from the family to go to college. I didn't know at this time whether or not I had won the scholarship.

I applied and got accepted for admission to Emerson College in Multan. Not only this was one of the prestigious colleges in Pakistan, it was not very far from Kacha Khuh – about 40 miles. More importantly, it was accessible by the railroad as well as the highway, both of which passed through the middle of Kacha Khuh. I was thrilled but, frankly, also nervous. Would I measure up to the standards of such a reputable college? How would a village boy like me adjust to the life in a big city like Multan?

Chapter 6

Multan: The City of Saints

After getting admission to Emerson College in Multan, I made a trip to the city together with my Mom and brother Rab to look for a place to stay. We rented a small one-bedroom house with a compound yard in the back. The house location was ideal – about 30 minutes away by foot from the main college entrance. My mother had brought along some kitchen stuff and it didn't take her long to set up an outdoor makeshift stove by stacking together a few bricks. Cots were furnished with the house and we had brought some bedding along. A general merchandise store was nearby to buy groceries and other essentials.

On the morning of my first day at college, I was excited but also nervous. I had heard that freshmen were subjected to hazing (we called it foolery) as they entered the college gate. I talked to Rab about my anxiety. He said he would accompany me to the gate and stand guard outside. Because no one except students was allowed to enter the college premises, he said he would yell from outside the gate if any one tried foolery on me. I felt a little reassured. As it turned out, I was able to sneak by the hazing bullies without an incident and Rab didn't have to yell.

As I walked through the college hallways, I saw students looking at their class schedules posted on the wall board. I jotted down my schedule and the room numbers for my classes. After that I had to find the rooms. It took a while to familiarize myself with all that. I entered my first classroom and took my seat. After a few minutes, the professor (called lecturer) came in, fully garbed in his academic robe. After a brief introduction, he called in the roll call by numbers. Each student registered for the first two years of college was assigned a roll number based on his standing in the past matriculation exam. My roll number was 17. That means there were 16 other enrollees who had scored higher than me in the national exam.

Prior to my college enrollment, I had thought of going into engineering. Accordingly, I registered for the pre-engineering courses: Physics, Math, Chemistry, and English (English was a compulsory subject). Also, the medium of instruction in college was English, which was a change from the high school. I had no problem with that because I liked to practice speaking English with my brothers Shah and Z.A. when they were home on vacations. Another change that I noticed had to do with classroom manners – if you wanted to leave the classroom for any reason, you didn't have to get teacher's permission. In college, it seemed, you were treated as adults – Yay!

I was happy that Mom was taking care of cooking and cleaning. Not far from us, there was a big house – a mansion belonging to a rich family. I struck up a friendship with a boy from that family and we would often play together in the front yard of his house. His parents treated me well and often invited me into their luxuriously furnished parlor. They were appreciative of my helping their kid in his school work (he was in high school).

Mom was always a very social person and it didn't take her long to make several friends in the neighborhood, including the rich family. When I would come home after school and didn't find Mom home, I would immediately assume that she was with her neighborhood lady friends. A side benefit for me of her sociability was that we would often get treats from her friends.

A few months after my college enrollment, I got a letter informing me that I had won the merit scholarship in my matriculation exam. The scholarship was for two years and would include free tuition and a stipend to cover my dormitory room and board. I decided to stay in the dorm. Mom had to say good bye to her friends in Multan and go back home to Kacha Khuh. Thank you Mom (in memory) for your love and support when I needed it the most!

The college dorm I moved into was called Tomlinson Hostel. It was located in the back premises of Emerson College. It had a nice gate that opened on to a wide open courtyard. The dorm rooms, with verandas, surrounded the courtyard on three sides. The hostel had a kitchen, dining hall, and a recreation room equipped with a ping pong table. Laundry service was provided by outside vendors who would regularly visit the dorm to collect and deliver laundry. I shared my room with two other students. The room was just big enough for three cots. During the summer nights, we set up our cots and beds out in the courtyard. Overall, the dorm accommodation was not luxurious but it was great for a village boy like me. What I liked the most about dorm life was the experience of living among my peers. It was experiencing college life to its fullest.

The first year of my college was mostly about getting used to the college environment: teachers, students, and dorm life. It left little time to explore things off-campus. However, I did familiarize myself with the nearby restaurants, bookstore, barber shop, and other places that catered to students. On weekends, I loved going to a cinema house and, once in a while, hang out with friends in the famous Multan Fort and the adjacent park. Other than that, it was mostly my books and me.

Multan is an ancient city, going back more than 5,000 years in history. It is called the city of saints because of a large collection of mausoleums belonging to *Sufi* saints (Islamic mystics). The shrines, with their elegant architecture, are magnets for the believers as well as tourists. Before you enter a mausoleum, you are greeted by a crowd of beggars and invalids, asking for alms. As you go inside, you are required to take off your shoes as a sign of respect for the saint buried there. The faithful would raise their hands and pray to God for the soul of the saint as well as for their own salvation. If you liked, you could also donate money to the custodians of the shrine for its maintenance and day-to-day upkeep.

Because of its history and antiquity, tourism thrives in Multan. Some of the favorite tourist places are the Multan Fort, historic city gates, and numerous shops selling pottery and handicrafts, unique to Multan as well as Pakistan. During four years of my stay in Multan, I had the opportunity to visit only a few of these sites. I was a student, not a tourist. I did visit Multan again in the year 2000 with my wife and children. This was a nostalgic experience for me to see the old places where I had spent four of my teenage years.

After my first year at Emerson, I felt confident in my studies. I liked my classes and the teachers, especially my physics professor. He would explain the physical concepts slowly and clearly, often giving examples from commonly observed phenomena. In the lab, he would help us devise simple experiments to verify physics laws and concepts. I give him a lot of credit for nurturing my early love for physics.

At the end of two years, I took the FSc (Faculty in Science) exam. I passed the exam as well as won another two-year merit scholarship. This was great news for me and my family. At least financially, the next two years of my college were assured!

After obtaining the FSc degree with pre-engineering courses, I had the pre-requisites for admission to Engineering school. But my heart was now set on physics instead. So, I decided to pursue a BSc degree, with courses in Physics, Math, Chemistry, and English. Realizing that math was an essential tool of physics, I registered for additional higher level math courses required for a BSc (Hons) degree - with Honors in Mathematics.

Based on the FSc exam scores, my new roll number in the class was 1. From then on, I was addressed as Number 1 by my teachers and frequently by my peers. I must admit I felt like a mini celebrity!

Thanks to the scholarship, I could stay on in the dorm for the remaining two years. The hostel was so close to where my classes were held that I would go to my dorm when there was a vacant period between classes. On weekends, my favorite place to study was the college pavilion which was next door and furnished with tables and benches. It was such a convenient, quiet, and cool place to study.

During my last year, I also participated in several extracurricular activities: debates, sports, and tabletop games. Prizes were awarded at the commencement to the winners in academics as well as extracurricular activities. I received a number of prizes both in academics and sports but the most coveted prize was the "best all-rounder award." I couldn't believe my ears when the announcer called my name; and then there was a cheering applause followed by a standing ovation. Wow, how could that be? It was an indescribable feeling!

At the end of four years at Emerson, I took the BSc (Hons) final exam. After the exam, I went home to await the results. After a few weeks, the results were published in the newspaper. I passed the exam but my score was not high enough to assure a merit scholarship. I later found out that I missed the cut-off score for a scholarship by a few points. I was very disappointed. Without a scholarship, I wasn't sure if my family could afford to send me to graduate school.

I had planned all along to pursue my MSc degree in physics. I talked to my family about it and then the head-scratching began. My father was adamant that I must continue my education until I had obtained the highest degree (as he had predicted). Pretty soon everybody agreed with Dad. I applied for admission to Government College Lahore and was accepted for the MSc program in physics, with nuclear physics as major. I also got admission to the dorm, New Hostel, which was located on the Government College campus.

When everything was all set to go, I boarded the train bound for Lahore. The year was 1957 and I was eighteen – a young man determined to get the "highest degree."

Chapter 7

Lahore: The City of Learning and Culture

Admission to the Government College Lahore (currently called Government College University or GCU) was a dream come true for me. At the time, this college was reputed to be one of the best in Pakistan. Founded in 1864, it is one of the oldest institutions of higher learning. Some of the notable alumni include scholars such as Allama Iqbal (1877 – 1938), the National Poet of Pakistan, and Abdus Salam (1926 – 1996), a 1979 Nobel Laureate in physics.

When I got there in 1957, the physics department was headed by Dr. Rafi M. Chaudhry, a renowned nuclear physicist. He had received his PhD at the Cavendish Laboratory (England) under the supervision of a Nobel Laureate, Ernest Rutherford, the discoverer of alpha and beta particles. Dr. Chaudhry founded and directed the "High Tension Laboratory" in the tradition of the Cavendish Lab. I had the honor of being his student.

It was a great experience for me to stay at the New Hostel of GCU. Compared to Tomlinson Hostel in Multan, the New Hostel offered much better accommodations, such as choice of individual rooms, better bathrooms with showers, and availability of personal attendants for housekeeping and other valet services. Also, the residents were drawn from different parts of the country, thereby contributing to greater enrichment of social interactions.

Because I had no scholarship to help pay for the college and dorm expenses, I depended on my family assistance to finance my graduate school education. On my part, I was able to get a lab assistant job which came with free college tuition. That helped a bit but I still needed money to pay for the dorm and other living expenses. Thankfully, I received a monthly check from home on a regular basis to cover those costs. I greatly appreciate my family for their support at this crucial time in my life.

I received my MSc degree in physics from GCU in 1959. At that time, MSc was the highest degree available in Pakistan. My family was jubilant, especially my father who had predicted that someday I would get "the highest degree in the world". Well, I was still young enough to set my eyes on the world in order to achieve that goal!

Soon after graduating, I set out to look for a job. Going through newspaper ads became a daily routine. One day, I saw an ad for a lecturer's position at Forman Christian College (FCC) Lahore and I applied for it. After an interview, I was offered the position and I gladly accepted it. My job description included giving physics lectures as well as setting up lab experiments for the freshmen class. Because of my faculty position, I got faculty accommodations at Ewing Hall – the FCC hostel located in the Anarkali (Nila Gumbad) area. It was one of the most coveted areas to live.

The Ewing Hall is only steps away from the famous Anarkali bazaar, King Edwards Medical College, and the great Mall Road. This was an ideal location for me to explore the many wonders of Lahore. Most of my favorite places to visit were located along or within less than three miles from the Mall Road. Besides restaurants, shopping malls, and movie theaters that I frequented, there were many historic and cultural places at a walking distance such as Lahore Museum, Jinnah Garden, and Lahore Zoo. If you didn't feel like walking, you could hire a cab or a *tonga* (horse buggy) to visit places like Lahore Fort, Badshahi Mosque, and Shalimar

Gardens. Now that I wasn't a student anymore, I had more time to enjoy the social and cultural sites of Lahore.

To shop in Anarkali was always fun for me. This is a bazaar where the price tags don't mean a thing. Unless you are a novice, you have to haggle. The shopkeepers expect haggling and, therefore, mark the items two to three times higher than they are actually worth. For example, if you want something at a reasonable or, better yet, bargain price, you start way down in your offer. Anarkali merchants don't feel insulted if your offer is far lower than the asking price. Starting with your bottom offer, you gradually increase it. A bargain hunter would then make the final offer and start walking away. If the merchant still does not budge, then maybe your offer was too low. You could repeat the process or just move on, depending on how badly you need the item.

Another fun place to be was the Mall Road. It is one of the most famous roads in Lahore. Lining the Mall on both sides are some of the finest restaurants, five star hotels, upscale shopping centers, and many attractions of historic and cultural value. Numerous movie theaters are located on or close to the Mall. Although Urdu and Punjabi movies were locals' favorite, the theaters that carried them were always too crowded to get in without a hassle. So, I developed a taste for the English language films. My favorite theater was Regal Cinema located right alongside the Mall. There I watched some of the great Hollywood films. I developed a liking for character actors such as Marlon Brando, Anthony Quinn, Laurence Olivier, Tony Curtis, Sidney Poitier, Gregory Peck, and other great actors of the 50's films. It was through these films that I came to appreciate American culture. I aspired to visit America someday and, better yet, get my highest degree there!

I had three close friends in Lahore with whom I spent most of my free time with: Shaukat, Rashid, and Naqvi. I was closest to Shaukat. He was a law student but his heart was into arts, literature, and philosophy. I owe a lot to him for developing within me a sense of appreciation for the arts. I needed that to understand beauty and human emotions. Rashid was a language professor and a poet. Naqvi was an intellectual who had interest in government, politics, and everything else. The four of us would often get together to shoot the breeze as well as have serious discussions about art, science, and current affairs of the world.

Although I had a nice job at the FCC, I would often look at newspaper ads for positions that might better fit my qualifications and interests. In 1960, a position was advertised for a hospital physicist in Mayo Hospital Lahore. Attached to King Edwards Medical University, Mayo Hospital (built in 1870 and named after Lord Mayo, Viceroy of British India) is one of the most prestigious hospitals in Pakistan. The position required an MSc degree in physics. Until then, I had never heard of physicists working in hospitals. Because the job came with a much higher salary than I was getting as a lecturer at the FCC, I decided to apply for it. I was called in for an interview at a government office. When I got there, I saw several other candidates, including some of my classmates, waiting for the interview. I felt a little intimidated by the competition, but then I thought what did I have to lose. At least, I could fall back on my lecturer's job.

In the interview, I had no problem answering questions about my educational background and other info until one of the panel members asked me: "What is a roentgen?" After thinking a bit, I said something like: "I don't know exactly what it means but I think it has something to do with measurement of radiation."

After a few days, I got a letter informing me that I had been selected for the position. I was thrilled but still didn't have a clue what the job entailed. On the first day of work, I reported to my boss, Dr. Yaqub. He was the head of radiation therapy at Mayo Hospital. I instantly recognized him as the person who had asked me the "roentgen" question. He explained to me what my job would be. He also told me that I was the first hospital physicist hired in Pakistan. Wow! But, where would I get the job training? Dr. Yaqub pulled a couple of books out of his desk drawer and asked me to read them. The books were on radiation therapy physics, authored by some British hospital physicists that Dr. Yaqub knew. That meant I would be training myself on the job by reading the textbooks he gave me.

Dr. Yaqub was trained as a radiation oncologist (then called radiotherapist) in England where hospital physicists worked side by side with the physicians in radiotherapy. His familiarity with the role of physicists in radiotherapy helped me understand my responsibilities.

Dr. Yaqub asked me to set up my desk in the corner of his office and took me under his wings from then on. He often took me along when he saw his patients. He would even ask me to wear a surgery gown and accompany him to the operating room where he administered radium implants to his patients. That helped me greatly to get acclimatized to the clinical environment. After a few months of self-training on the job under Dr. Yaqub's guidance, I began to catch on with my role as a hospital physicist.

Our department at the time had a couple of x-ray therapy machines; one for treating superficial cancers and the other for deep-seated tumors. From the books and manuals, I learned how to measure radiation dose and calibrate the x-ray machines. I used the dosimeter (Victoreen R-meter) that was available in our department. Besides dosimetry, I also familiarized myself with setting up patients on the treatment couch and operating the x-ray machines by working with the therapy technicians who administered the treatments.

After about a year on the job, in 1961, our new department under construction got completed and was ready to move in. The new department, called the Institute of Radiotherapy, was well-equipped, considering existing standards. Most importantly, the department had acquired a brand new cobalt-60 teletherapy machine, probably the first in Pakistan. This machine, invented in 1951 by a Canadian medical physicist, Harold E. Johns (1915 – 1998), was a revolutionary advance in radiotherapy. It produced a well-collimated gamma ray beam which could be directed at the patient's tumor from different directions to destroy it, while sparing as much as possible the skin and normal tissue surrounding the tumor. The cobalt machine was the main radiation treatment modality in the world until the 1970's when linear accelerators started to become the mainstay of radiotherapy.

I observed the installation and testing of our cobalt machine by the vendor engineer. As I was the institution's physicist, it was my responsibility to check and calibrate the machine for radiation output before it could be used to treat patients. But the problem was that I was not familiar with the protocol for calibrating a cobalt unit. We waited until a Swiss hospital physicist, under the sponsorship of an international organization (probably IAEA), was invited by Dr. Yaqub to visit our department. He calibrated our cobalt machine and went over with me about other procedures to check its performance accuracy. I soaked up all that information like a sponge.

After the Swiss physicist left, I trained myself well enough to get a green light from Dr. Yaqub to start treating patients. From then on, I was made responsible to treat cobalt patients on a daily basis. At one time, I was treating about 15 – 20 patients a day. This arrangement continued until I trained the therapy technicians to take over the responsibility.

About a year after moving into our new department, Dr. Yaqub retired and a new radiation oncologist, Dr. S. M. Masood, took his place. Dr. Masood was also a British trained radiation oncologist and was familiar with the role of hospital physicists. So, we worked together closely as a team. By now, I was well-versed in planning cobalt and radium treatments. I would do the treatment plans manually (computers were unheard of then) and show it to Dr. Masood for his approval. This routine was followed for each patient. As ours was a teaching hospital, I also trained the medical residents to do some of the plans as a teaching exercise.

When I was working at Mayo, I had rented an apartment in the YMCA, located on the Mall Road and at a walking distance from the hospital. It was a nice place to live not only because of its location but also the amenities it offered such as an in-house restaurant and clean bathrooms and showers. With a reasonably descent salary now, I could afford to live at a hip place like this!

My working hours in our department were from 7:00 AM to 3:00 PM. The basement of our department had a few rooms furnished with beds and a shower for the staff to take an afterwork siesta if they so desired. Call that a perk? After taking a short afternoon nap and shower, I was ready for gallivanting with my friends. It was almost a routine for the two or three of us to take a walk on the Mall road, have snack at a restaurant (Shezan was our favorite), and end up at the Jinnah Garden. An open-air restaurant there was another favorite of ours to chat over a cup of tea (Samosas were delicious there.)

My friend, Shaukat, had a deep influence intellectually on me. It was because of him that I began to appreciate art and literature. In a few years that I was associated with him, I had read Shakespeare, Oscar Wilde, Baudelaire, Emilie Zola, Balzac, Tennessee Williams, Steinbeck, Dostoyevsky, Tolstoy, and several other great authors. Both of us became member of the Alhambra Art Council, located on the Mall Road, and would often go there to visit art galleries and exhibits. Other big attractions there were the classical dance and music events. Alhambra was and still is the cultural heart of Lahore.

Shaukat also loved photography. With a classic camera, Franka Solida, in his hand, he would go into city neighborhoods to take snapshots of life as it existed. He was a documentary photographer. He called photography a medium of expression and the camera an instrument of truth. It was not long before his passion for photography began to rub on me, too. So, I bought a Franka Solida and began to learn the technique of picture taking and processing photography prints in Shaukat's dark room lab at his home. Just like Shaukat, I would go into neighborhoods to look for interesting subjects. You had to hide the camera behind your back so as not to startle the subject(s) in the scene. Pretty soon, photography became my main hobby. Shaukat introduced me also to the works of famous photographers: Edward Weston, Edward Steichen, Yousuf Karsh, Cartier Bresson, Ansel Adams, Dorthea Lange, and several others. *The Family of Man*, a book of photographic exhibition created by Edward Steichen for the Museum of Modern Art, New York, became my constant companion.

I stayed in Lahore for a total of six years. Based on my experience there, I would call it a great city of learning and culture. I still miss you Lahore!

Chapter 8

Goodbye Lahore, Hello Minneapolis

When I switched from pure physics to hospital physics (called medical physics nowadays), it was a career change for me. After a year or two of working in radiation therapy, I liked the field so much that I began to dream about going abroad someday where I could pursue advanced studies in the field. But I didn't have the faintest idea how that could be possible.

I thought dreams were just dreams until one day when I saw an ad in the paper about some American scholarships being offered to Pakistan under the Fulbright Scholarship Exchange Program. A total of twenty-eight scholarships were offered for the whole country (East and West Pakistan.) That included all fields of study. My chances of getting one looked pretty slim. But then I thought I would never know unless I tried it. So I went ahead and applied for it.

I got a little bit excited when I received a letter to appear for interview; the dream got a little more vivid. Outside the interview office, I saw a long line of candidates waiting. That meant the competition for the scholarships was intense. Well, after initial nervousness, it didn't matter. It was just an interview like any other. When my name was called, I felt confident. The interview panel consisted of several people, including a couple of Americans, presumably from the U.S. embassy. After asking questions about my educational background, the panelists showed curiosity about my job as a hospital physicist. I explained my job with enthusiasm and stressed my desire to pursue advanced studies in the area of cancer treatment by radiation.

One of the American panelists (a lady) asked me about my hobbies. I said it was photography. Then she asked if I had seen a photography exhibit lately. I said yes. I told her about my membership of the Alhambra Art Council and that I had recently seen the work of Ansel Adams exhibited there. Then I commented on how great the exhibit was. By now, I could discern an expression of delight on her face.

After the interview, I felt good but not overly optimistic. The time passed and I got immersed in my hospital job as before. Then one day, I got this letter from the U.S. embassy. I couldn't believe my eyes: I had been selected for the Fulbright Scholarship. A couple of friends were in my room at the time. I started jumping up and down, saying I got it, I got it. Finally, when I simmered down a little, I told my friends the big news. Then we all started jumping and screaming with joy.

After the celebration was over, the teasing began. How would it feel to sink my teeth into pig's meat? I kept saying: no, no, it won't happen; Americans have other meats also like beef and chicken. Shaukat said something like: oh yeah? What about kissing girls on the lips, smeared with pork? That thought had never occurred to me until then.

A week or two later, I got a package from the US IIE (Institute of International Education) containing several forms to fill out. My boss, Dr. Masood, was kind enough to help me fill them out. Besides my detailed CV and other pertinent information, I had to designate my field of study. Although the scholarship was for one year, I made a case for enrolling in a PhD program in biophysics.

After several months of waiting, I got the final papers: I had been admitted to a PhD program in biophysics at the University of Minnesota. My advisor for the program would be Dr. Otto Schmitt. I would be reporting to Dr. Alfred Nier, Chairman of the Physics Department at the University of Minnesota. All travel arrangement had been made by the IIE, including a check to cover expenses during travel. There would be a car waiting for me to pick me up when I arrive at the New York and Minneapolis airports. Come to think of it now, that was a treatment fit for a royalty. Thanks in advance, IIE!

The first order of business now was to find out where the heck Minnesota was. I went to the American Center library and there I found Minnesota on the map. I made sure it was part of the USA, not Canada.

Now the ordeal of getting the passport began. Pakistan was, and still is, one of the biggest bureaucracies in the world. My employment at the Mayo (a government hospital) made it even more complicated. I had to get permission from the Secretariat of Health. I waited and waited, but no response. Apparently the health department was not in a hurry. After I got really fed up, I got one of our staff doctors to help me in this struggle. Apparently he talked to someone and I was finally called for interview with a person in charge of my case. As I entered his office, he politely asked me what was the hangup. I told him that I was going to America on a Fulbright Scholarship and that it would not involve any expenses or obligations to the government of Pakistan. Then, I unloaded all of my pent-up frustration about the delay. The man acted cool as a cucumber. He listened and then gently said: Ok, you can go now.

I came out of the office and sat down on a bench nearby to collect myself. After a few minutes, the man came out of his office and said to me: Simmer down young man; I have approved your passport application. I was simply flabbergasted!

On the day of the departure from Lahore, my parents and other family members showed up at the airport to say goodbye. Tears were flowing freely. I waved goodbye to them before boarding the plane. When the plane took off, I peeked through the window: Goodbye, dear Lahore!

I had an overnight layover in Karachi. I had a voucher to stay at the airport hotel and depart for New York the next morning. When I arrived at the hotel, I felt like throwing up. That is when I experienced my first air sickness. I never had a plane ride before.

In the evening I ventured out of my room to have a bite to eat. The hotel restaurant was serving buffet with all sorts of good food. I looked at the food but felt nauseated again. I came back to my room and lay down in my bed, exhausted. I fell asleep. When I got up, I felt a little better. My flight had to leave early in the morning. I boarded the plane and soon the plane took off. I still felt ok. Apparently, I had gotten over my air sickness. Thank goodness!

The plane landed in New York sometime around noon. As I came outside of the passenger area, I saw a man from the IIE holding a sign with my name. He had a car waiting outside to take me to the hotel. My flight to Minneapolis was scheduled to take off next morning. The driver got me registered at the hotel and left. I rested in my room for a while and then decided to check out the famous New York. Wow! All I could see outside were skyscrapers lining both sides of the road. It surely looked different than the Lahore Mall Road.

My friend Shaukat had asked me to go to the Magnum Photo Gallery in New York and find out the status of his prints that he had submitted for possible publication in a photo magazine. With the address in hand, I followed the avenue to get to the street where the place was located. After a long walk I found the Magnum. I went in and talked to a person at the desk about Shaukat's prints. They showed me his photos but none had been chosen for publication. Sorry, Shaukat.

I also wanted to visit the famous Museum of Modern Arts, where the photography exhibit, The Family of Man, was on display. From the Magnum Gallery, the museum wasn't too far. When I got there, it was closed because it was Monday. Oh, shucks. Then I ventured into a restaurant. I was craving for some spicy food. I picked up a fillet of fish, breaded and deep-fried golden brown. It looked appetizing. But when I took a bite, it was tasteless. Then I tried a dark-chocolate bar. Instead of being sweet like candy, it tasted kind a bitter. Welcome to the American food!

I came back to the hotel, rested a while, and then fell asleep. Early in the morning, I was startled out of my sleep by a loud banging noise. I got up to look out the window. There I saw big trucks hauling garbage cans. The ruckus continued for a while and that was the end of my sleep.

After the garbage trucks left, it was time to get ready for my flight to Minneapolis. The hotel attendant knocked at my door and told me that my ride to the airport was waiting outside. It took a while for us to commute through heavy traffic, but we made it to the airport on time. I boarded the plane, got settled in my seat, and started thinking about Minneapolis: Is it like New York, with rows of skyscrapers or like Lahore with the expansive Mall Road, shopping centers, and beautiful gardens?

When the plane got to Minnesota, I looked out the window. I couldn't believe my eyes: A landscape studded with green and colorful trees and stretches of water here and there. Gorgeous!

The plane landed at the Minneapolis airport. It was midmorning of September 10, 1963. Hello, Minneapolis!

I got picked up at the airport by the IIE car and taken to an apartment house in Dinkytown – a campus town next door to the University of Minnesota. There I met a group of Pakistani students who welcomed me to stay with them temporarily until I could find a place of my own. Apparently, this was pre-arranged by the IIE.

The next day, I was supposed to report to the foreign students' registration office, located in Eddy Hall on the U of M campus. There the staff helped me with everything I needed to do to get registered, meet my academic advisor, and find housing. While I was taking care of my paperwork, I met a Pakistani student, Ashraf. Together, we found a house to rent in Dinkytown. The upstairs was already rented out and we rented the downstairs.

Back at the foreign students' office, I had also received directions to the physics department to meet my academic advisor. I went there and met Dr. Nier, the department Chair. I showed him my papers and had a brief chat with him. He directed me to another building where I could meet my assigned academic advisor, Dr. Otto Schmitt, the head of the biophysics department. As I entered his office, I saw Dr. Schmitt sitting behind his desk with piles of papers and folders. It was the messiest desk I had ever seen!

Right after I introduced myself, Dr. Schmitt pulled out his Polaroid camera and took my picture. Then he asked me to sit down. I went over with him about my background and explained to him my desire to pursue a PhD program in biophysics. I also talked to him about my interest in the field of radiation therapy physics. He told me that one of his former students, Dr. Merle Loken, who was the head of nuclear medicine at the time, had the right qualifications to advise me in what I wanted to do. So, he called him on the phone and made an appointment for me to see him.

At this point let me take a moment to say few words about Dr. Schmitt. Otto Herbert Schmitt (1913 – 1998) was a world renowned biophysicist and innovator. He founded the Biophysics Lab at the University of Minnesota. Among his numerous contributions to biophysics and biomedical engineering, he is best known for inventing Schmitt trigger. This electronic circuitry allows conversion of a constant electronic signal to an on/off state. Nowadays it is used in millions of electronic devices, including computers. I was not aware of Dr. Schmitt's accomplishments as a scientist until later. That information came from those who knew about him and his contributions.

As directed by Dr. Schmitt, I met Dr. Loken and explained to him my primary interest in clinical radiation therapy physics. He understood exactly what my goal was and told me that he would be glad to be my academic advisor. After looking at my educational resume, he planned out my PhD program in biophysics with courses drawn from several fields: biology, physics, math, physical chemistry, biochemistry, biophysics, and radiological physics. In the end, it turned out to be about 125 credits worth of didactic coursework, followed by a PhD thesis. To Dr. Loken, time to finish the degree was not an issue; comprehensiveness of the program was the main objective. On my part, I just wanted to get started and keep on going as long as I was able to stay in the U.S. My scholarship was for one year but that did not deter me from pursuing my ultimate goal – a PhD degree. May be I could get a job after the scholarship ended. I was used to daydreaming!

As my academic program got started, I settled in my new place. While Ashraf and I shared the downstairs, the upstairs was occupied by a nice couple, Carl and Rosemary. Carl was a graduate student in arts at the U. It was not long before I became friends with the couple. I would often get together with the couple upstairs and talk about art, photography, and other subjects of common interest. As long as I stayed there, I greatly enjoyed the company of Carl and Rosemary.

My first year in America was a learning process about American food and culture. For example, when I visited a snack shop in Dinkytown, I saw food packages labeled as "hot dog." I was perplexed. Do Americans eat dog meat? The misunderstanding was soon cleared up when the shop attendant explained that it was pork. Oh, well, I couldn't eat it anyway. Another example: On the first day of my class, I found myself to be the only one wearing a suit and tie. Everybody else was in casuals. Some were even in worn-out jeans. From then on, I followed the adage: When in Rome, do as the Romans do.

More challenging than the food and the dress code was the adjustment to Minnesota weather. During my first winter, I was not well-prepared for the cold wind. One day, I had to walk to my class across campus. It was a long walk and I had to pass by a couple of tall buildings. Suddenly, I got caught in a cold blast from a wind tunnel. I was wearing a warm jacket but nothing to protect my face and ears from the biting wind. Finally, as I got into the building where my class was being held, I sat down on a bench and broke down into tears. "What am I doing here?" I asked myself. All kinds of thoughts crossed my mind: home, family, purpose of my trip, and so on. Then, I composed myself with a fresh determination. I was not going back without accomplishing what I came to do.

In midwinter, I saw the first snowfall. It was beautiful – more beautiful than what I had seen in the movies. I also learned, from the couple upstairs, that we had to take turns in shoveling the snow off the sidewalk in the front of the house. No problem, as long as you cleaned the path right after the snow fall. It is no fun to walk on Icy walkways. Nonetheless, coming from a hot desert climate where it never snowed, the spectacle was great to watch. Shoveling snow was no big deal.

As the summer approached, I started looking for a summer job. The scholarship funding was getting close to its end. I went to the Mayo Clinic for an interview, but the job had already been promised to someone else before I got there. I came back disappointed but then I thought I should talk to my advisor about my financial predicament. He advised me to apply for extension of my Fulbright scholarship. He wrote a strong letter in support of my request. He based his recommendation on the fact that I was making good progress towards my PhD program and that my going back to Pakistan after one year would be a waste of effort already expended in that regard. The IIE graciously extended my scholarship for one more year, with the stipulation that I had to be self-supporting thereafter in order to continue my studies. I thanked the IIE and my lucky stars!

With the scholarship extended, I felt like moving to a better place to live. I rented a one bedroom efficiency apartment in a two-story rooming house in the heart of Dinkytown. The room was furnished with a bed and an electric stove. Each floor had a common bathroom. I liked the place because of its close proximity to the U campus as well as the Dinkytown neighborhood with several restaurants, shops, and a movie theater. I joined a diner club close by, which was very convenient for students like me who don't have much time to cook their daily meals.

By the end of first year as a student, I felt well-adjusted to the campus life. There were social groups on campus who would take foreign students on excursions and other activities such as picnics, social gatherings, and visiting American families. That helped a lot in assimilating foreign students into the American way of life.

In the rooming house I was staying, I struck friendship with an American student, named Ed. Once he took me to his home in the countryside where I spent a weekend with him and his family. Their house was on a farm. At night, I heard strange sounds coming from outside the house. The next morning, I asked Ed about it. He explained that it must be the pigs. I had never seen a pig before so I accompanied him to the pigpen. Although Muslims consider pigs as "unclean" animals, I got over my inhibition and helped Ed to carry water and buckets of food over to the pigs. I enjoyed the whole experience.

While most of my time was spent attending classes at the U, I had a pretty good social life after the school hours. There were many Indian and Pakistani students living in Dinkytown to hang around with in the evenings and on weekends. At night, we would sometimes walk over to the night clubs downtown. Those days, there was no fear of being mugged while walking downtown at night!

I loved going to the movies. I had acquired the habit in Lahore. The Varsity Theater in Dinkytown was a few blocks from my rooming house. I don't think I missed any new movie that was shown there. I also acquired the taste for pizza. Earl's Pizza in Dinkytown was my favorite. McDonald's hamburger with french fries wasn't bad either. Ice cream at Bridgeman was a great treat. With all the activities and great food, Dinkytown was the place to be at this time of my life. In a way, it acted like an antidote for my homesickness.

In the spring of 1965, I started looking for a job. My second year of scholarship was about to expire. I talked to a few people in the radiology department at the U about the possibility of a job there. I got an appointment to see the head of the radiation therapy division, Dr. Giulio D'Angio. In the interview, he asked me about my educational background and any experience in radiotherapy. I went over everything I had learned and done at the Mayo Hospital, Lahore. He got particularly interested in my experience with planning radium implants. He asked me if I would be interested in working on a project that he had in mind regarding the use of radium implants and cobalt teletherapy in the treatment of cervix cancer. With great enthusiasm I said yes. He hired me right on the spot. I started the job as a dosimetrist in June of 1965.

At this juncture, it felt like I was going to fulfill my career aspirations. My great thanks to America for the Fulbright scholarship and Dr. D'Angio for the first job!

Chapter 9

Finding Love

The rooming house I was living in was co-ed. The women lived downstairs and the men upstairs. Once in awhile, the residents got together for a party. Everybody knew each other. Most of them were students. The gentleman living across my room was an elderly man who had a strange habit of tinkering with his iron-frame bed at night. His hammering and rattling drove me crazy. I complained about it to the caretaker but to no avail. Adding insult to injury, the old man owned a dog that was tied up by the garage in the backyard, right outside my window. Between the old man's tinkering and his dog's whimpering, it became impossible to stay in that room. So, I moved to another room, still upstairs but close to the front of the house, where I could not hear the noises. In spite of all that, I liked the house and the friendliness of its residents.

Downstairs, at the entrance of the house, a pretty girl, named Kathy Boer, had her apartment – a narrow kitchen on the left and a bedroom across on the right of the entry way. If she was working in her kitchen, I would often stop by to say hello to her. Not only was she beautiful, it was very nice to talk to her. I got to know her a little better during house parties. I don't know what she thought of me, but I felt kind of attracted to her. This feeling stayed dormant until one evening I saw her studying in the

Diehl Hall University Library. I went over to her and said hi as usual. We talked for a while, in a hushed tone of voice of course to meet the library decorum, and then decided to walk back to the house together. Outside, across the street from the library, we stopped and looked into each other's eyes. In a trembling voice, I asked: Can I kiss you? She said yes and closed her eyes. I kissed her and she kissed me back. I felt I was on cloud 9!!!

The first kiss gave way to dating and knowing each other. Going to the movies, Earl's Pizza, Vescio's Italian restaurant, and Bridgeman's ice cream, were frequent places to enjoy food and each other's company. We started dating sometime in 1965. By 1966, I was ready to propose. She accepted!!!

She invited her parents, who lived in Iowa, to visit us. They came over and took us to dinner. I liked her parents. After they left, I asked Kathy about what they thought of me. She said that her dad was fine but her mom had some reservations (typical of moms!).

We planned to have two marriage ceremonies: one according to the Muslim tradition and the other Christian. The Muslim wedding was held in our rooming house, on February 18, 1966. I asked a few Muslim student friends to be present and one of them, with a long beard (hallmark of a *Maulvi* or Muslim scholar), conducted the ceremony. It simply required the bride and the groom to agree to a marriage contract in the presence of at least two witnesses. Verses from the Holly Qur'an were recited to ask God's blessing on the marriage.

A formal church wedding was held the following day. As Kathy's dad walked her down the aisle, the organ music of Johann Sebastian Bach (played on request) sounded beautiful. The marriage vows were exchanged. I had found my love. She turned out to be the love of my life!!!

After the wedding, we left for Lake Okoboji in Iowa for our honeymoon. Kathy's parents had a cabin right on the lake. The lake, the privacy, a record player (Westinghouse gramophone), and the two of us together – It couldn't get better than that!

Now that we were married, we had to move out of the rooming house. We found an apartment a few blocks away but still in Dinkytown. At this time, Kathy was working fulltime in a law firm as a secretary. She worked for two prominent attorneys, Harry MacLaughlin and Blaine Harstad. The former would become Justice of the Minnesota Supreme Court in 1972 and U.S. District Court judge in 1977.

Between Kathy's working at the law firm and my job at the U, we were doing OK financially. She had a car to commute to work and I biked back and forth from the U. I could even afford to buy her a gift, a bracelet, on her birthday. She bought me a Hasselblad camera I had always wanted. The camera was lot more expensive than the bracelet but who cares when you are in love?

Kathy was expecting and we were both thrilled at the thought of having a baby in our lives. What should be his/her name? We decided that the first name should be American and the second name Pakistani. Accordingly, when the baby girl was born, we picked her name to be Sarah Kalsoom. Although Sarah is a popular name in America, a version of it, Sara, is also a Pakistani name. In either case, Sarah is derived from the name of the Prophet Abraham's wife (Sarah in the Bible and Sara in the Qur'an). Kalsoom is a Pakistani name, after Umme Kulsoom, the granddaughter of the Prophet Muhammad.

Sarah was a beautiful baby and had a very cheerful disposition. She would smile broadly at the slightest hint of baby talk. As the first child, our life revolved around her. As a dad, all I cared most about was hugging, cuddling, and playing with her. For her mom, it was lot more than just fun: like holding her and soothing her when she cried, feeding her, bathing her, and keeping her diapers clean. She even taught me how to swish the dirty cloth diapers in the toilet. She expected me to share some of the child-rearing duties. I had no choice!

Meanwhile, I was doing well in my studies and my work in the radiation therapy department. I was getting on-the-job training under Vaughn Moore, the Chief Physicist in the department at that time. He was a board-certified radiological physicist and also a PhD student in biophysics. Dr. Loken was the academic advisor for both of us. I was so lucky to work with people like Dr. D'Angio, Dr. Loken, and Vaughn Moore at this juncture of my career.

Remember (from the last chapter) that Dr. D'Angio had assigned me a research project related to the radiation treatment of cervix cancer. I completed that project and presented the results in a joint meeting of the radiation therapy and GYN departments. At the end of my talk, Dr. D'Angio complimented me about the work and recommended that the department stop using the existing technique (which I maintained was obsolete and fraught with radiation induced complications). From that time on the department adopted the "Fletcher technique," which I had found to be a safer method of delivering radiation to a cervix tumor. Subsequent to my completion of the project, I wrote my findings up as a term paper. I got an A for it!

When I joined the department in 1965, I had been carrying a full load of course work as well as my job responsibilities in the clinic. I also found time to work on research that could possibly lead to my PhD dissertation. During that time, the University acquired a mainframe computer, the Control Data CDC 3300. It was installed in the University Hospital. Both Vaughn Moore and I got interested in computer programming. We took formal courses in the FORTRAN programming language. Vaughn subsequently was able to finish his PhD thesis using his computer program as a tool.

When Vaughn got his PhD, I was still working on my course work and research for a possible PhD thesis project. After finishing all the required courses, I had to take my preliminary oral exam in order to get the formal designation of a Candidate for PhD. This is considered to be the toughest exam of the whole graduate program. You have to pass this exam before you can proceed with your PhD thesis research.

My examining panel consisted of professors drawn from the physics, physical chemistry, and biophysics departments, in addition to my academic advisor, Dr. Loken. The biophysics professor on the panel was no other than Dr. Otto Schmitt.

It was a custom then, and I think it still is, that the candidate would provide coffee and cookies for the panel (presumably, to put the examiners in a favorable mood). So I did what I was told by those who had preceded me in taking such an exam.

One thing good about my panel was that I knew the professors well – I had taken their courses in my graduate studies. I was familiar with their favorite topics and I had especially prepared for them. As the exam proceeded, I felt confident that I was doing OK with the physics and physical chemistry questions. I also noticed that Dr. Schmitt was taking catnaps off and on during this time. When it was his turn, he seemed to be wide-awake. He asked me questions on electrocardiography and efficiency of a heart pump. Some of them I answered Ok but some I struggled through a bit. At the end, I was asked to wait outside the room in order for the panel to deliberate. After a short wait, Dr. Loken came out and said "Congratulations!" For a moment I thought of jumping up with excitement but, instead, shook hands and thanked him profusely. Then I entered the room and shook hands with all members of the panel.

Now that I was officially a candidate for PhD, I focused on my thesis work. I had already done some experiments related to methods and devices for modifying a cobalt beam profile in order to deliver a uniform radiation dosage to the tumor. I came up with a device (called compensator) that could be custom-designed for an individal patient. I also solved the attendant problem of what is called the "electron contamination" of the photon beam in order to minimize adverse skin reaction in the treated area of the patient. The device I came up with is known as the "electron filter." I published my first paper on these topics in a peer-reviewed journal, Radiology, in 1968.

I got most of my ideas for thesis research from my work in the clinic. I worked closely with the physicians (radiation oncologists) in order to understand treatment problems that adversely affected their patients. For example, a new technique (called mantle field) for treating patients with Hodgkin's disease had been introduced at Stanford University and was being implemented in our department. The challenge was to calculate the dose received by the patient within the tumor-bearing areas as well as the surrounding normal tissues and organs at risk from radiation damage. I embarked on a project to solve this problem. I thought, if successful, I could possibly use it for my PhD dissertation.

It took me several months to work out the theory of modeling the cobalt beam. But the equations were too laborious for manual calculations. It is then that I decided to write a computer algorithm. I wrote the program in FORTRAN on punched cards, using a keypunch machine. After numerous trials and errors on the CDC computer and boxes full of punched cards, I was finally able to run the program successfully and error free.

The program was capable of calculating and displaying radiation dose distributions within a patient in three dimensions. I would input typical patient information on punched cards, run the program, and get the results back as a printout. I would then spot check the computer output by manual calculations. After numerous runs, debugging, and editing, I was able to finalize the program. It was now time to test the program experimentally.

Using a patient model (a tissue-equivalent body torso), I experimentally tested the program a sufficient number of times to establish its accuracy within acceptable statistical limits. I presented the results in a special department meeting as a rehearsal for my final exam. Their comments were positive.

I wrote up the thesis longhand because in those days my typing was atrocious. Moreover, I could not compose my thoughts as well when typing as I did writing longhand. Kathy, who is a great typist, came to the rescue. She typed up the whole 175-page thesis, except for the math equations and formulas, which I penned in longhand in black ink. When it was all done, I made several copies of the thesis for the exam committee.

The final exam was scheduled and the same exam committee was constituted as for my earlier prelim exam. This time I was expected to present my thesis research and defend it. I breezed through my presentation with confidence. After all, it was my research and I knew it more than anybody else on the committee. I got a number of questions during and after the presentation, but everything went well. At the end, I was asked, as usual, to leave the room while the committee deliberated and took a vote. As before, Dr. Loken came out and said: "CONGRATULATIONS"!!!

The first thing I did after the great news was to call my dear wife. She was thrilled; then more "CONGRATULATIONS" from her!!! While on the phone, I suggested casually that maybe I should pursue an MD degree because, with my PhD in biophysics, it would take me only two years to finish medical school rather than the regular four years. I could hear her crying on the phone. She told me she could not take two more years of my being a student. At this point, the message was clear; I never thought of pursuing my MD again.

A few weeks after the final exam, I got a telegram from my family in Pakistan, informing me that my father was severely ill. I immediately made my plane reservations and let my family know that I was on my way. The journey back home was very emotional for me. What would I say to my father when I saw him? I hoped he would be alive to hear me tell him that I had obtained the highest degree that he had predicted for me . . . Sorry, I am in tears right now as I am recalling that moment. I will continue later.

As my plane flew over Lahore, nostalgia took over me. Old memories of my days in Lahore brought tears in my eyes. After all, I had been away for 5 years. When the plane landed, it felt like home. As I exited the plane, I saw lots of people standing behind the fence and waving. As I walked up close, I saw a group of people shouting and waving towards me. I recognized some of them – my family members who had come to greet me at the airport. I met them at the exit gate. As I hugged my brother Z.A., I noticed sadness in his face. I asked him about Dad. In a barely audible voice, he said he had passed away. I hugged him again and we both cried. Then everybody took turns to greet me and console me.

Z.A. drove me in his car to Kacha Khuh where the rest of my family was waiting. I saw my mother with her arms open to hug me. It was a long hug, with my mother wailing loudly and everybody around us crying. Most of them were women relatives and neighbors who had gathered in our house to pay condolences. It is a custom among women to sit down in groups and wail in grief for the deceased.

The next morning, they took me to the graveyard where my father was buried. They showed me my father's grave. The grave next to father's belonged to my youngest sister, Alam Khatoon. She had died of complications from miscarriage when I had been away. I sat down by both graves and cried.

It was nice to spend a few weeks with my family; meeting relatives and old friends in Kacha Khuh and Chak 29. It seemed things had barely changed since I had left. I spent a lot of time with my mother. She gave me a full diary of family affairs, for example, which members of the family had treated her well and which ones had not. My mother always had her favorites and not so favorites. I would listen to her stories as long as I could stay awake.

Another thing we talked about most was my marriage. Marrying outside the relatives, let alone an American, was unusual for my family. I showed them pictures of Kathy and baby Sarah. I heard lots of oohs and aahs for both. They liked my choice of Sarah's name, which they pronounced as Sa-ra.

One day, during my stay there, I got a letter from Kathy. I opened it in front of my mother. After I read it, my mother wanted to know what was said in the letter. I translated the letter, including the sentence, "I miss you." My mother retorted: "Not as much as I did." I laughed, but I also got the message that Kathy couldn't out do my mother in that respect!

Chapter 10

Family, Fun, and Frolic

My first trip back home since coming to America was both sad and exhilarating. It was sad because my father had passed away without knowing that his prediction of my getting the highest degree in the world had come true. It was exhilarating because I got to see my family and visit places where I was born and grew up.

After spending a few weeks in Pakistan, however, I felt homesick for America, just like I had felt home sick for Pakistan. I missed Kathy and baby Sarah. I couldn't wait to get back.

Although I had passed my final PhD exam in 1968, the diploma was to be awarded the following year in June at the commencement ceremony. On this day, the weather was sunny, hot, and humid. We were waiting on the front patio of the Northrop Auditorium and I was sweating like a trooper in my doctoral cap and gown. Kathy had her hands full with our high-energy toddler, Sarah. She was having a ball running around. Then suddenly I noticed a puddle of liquid beside her. Apparently, she had peed right on the patio. Kathy hurried up to clean up the spot and soon things went back to normal. But I could not miss noticing smirks on a few onlookers' faces around us.

After receiving my doctorate degree, I was promoted to assistant professorship. Also, the promotion came with a significant raise in salary. That was very timely for us because Kathy was expecting our second child. We needed a bigger place to live. We found a house for sale in South East Minneapolis and made an offer on it. The offer was accepted. This was our first house (I would call it the Como House). It had a big living room, good size kitchen, 3 bedrooms upstairs, and a nice backyard. Location wise, it was close to the U and the Dinkytown. But most importantly, we could afford the house.

Kathy went into labor on a snowy December night. I drove her to a hospital in downtown Minneapolis. As we arrived at the hospital, I parked the car and opened the door for Kathy. She said wait; she couldn't move. I thought she was going to deliver right in the car. A few moments later she was able to get out of the car and we walked down to the hospital lobby. There I told the receptionist that my wife was going to have a baby. She said that's obvious! (Sounded like a smart aleck). Then they quickly wheeled Kathy into the delivery room. It didn't take long before she delivered a healthy and beautiful baby.

We named our newborn Yasmine Joyce. Kathy and I had decided that the second child would have a Pakistani first name and American second name. I had picked the name Yasmine, after Princess Yasmine, the daughter of Prince Ali Khan and his wife Rita Hayworth, a famous American actress. Now we had our own little princess!

While Kathy was working full time taking care of our new baby and a demanding toddler, I was busy with my department work. We had our first medical linear accelerator delivered in 1969. At the time, this was a state-of-the-art radiation therapy machine. Unlike cobalt, which produces a gamma ray beam, a linear accelerator is capable of producing high-energy beams of X-rays as well as electrons. Because of this dual modality, it can be used to treat both superficial and deep-seated cancers.

The linear accelerator took several months to install, check, and commission for clinical use. Dr. Vaughn Moore (chief physicist at the time), the vendor engineer, and I worked long hours every day to get the machine ready for patient treatments. On my part, I took this opportunity to learn and research the new technology in as much depth as I could.

Another development of consequence happened in 1970. My favorite physician and boss, Dr. D'Angio, left and went to Cornell University, N.Y. In his place, Dr. Seymour Levitt was hired as the head of radiation therapy division. Not only was he an accomplished radiation oncologist, he was a great administrator. From his staff, he demanded dedication to high level of clinical service, research, and teaching. And these happened to be my ideals as well. So, he and I developed a great rapport.

In 1973, Dr. Moore left and I was offered the position of Director of Radiation Physics which I accepted. The following year, I was nominated for promotion to Associate Professor. The University Tenure Committee reviewed my CV and granted me the promotion. It was great because it provided me the security of being a tenured faculty, meaning that my position was permanent and could be terminated only under extraordinary circumstances, as defined in the University tenure code.

The year 1974 was a very good year for me. I was granted the citizenship of the United States of America. Being an American citizen has been a source of great pride for me ever since. I hope I have made, and would continue to make, contributions to America that are worthy of the honor it bestowed on me.

Until 1972, we stayed in our Como house. But as our finances improved, we started looking for a better home for our kids. We found a house that would meet the criteria. This house was located in Lauderdale, a close-in suburb of St. Paul. It was not very far from the U of MN Minneapolis and St. Paul campuses. Most importantly, the street it was on had lots of kids of about the same age as our kids. This house turned out to be where we raised all our kids. For them, it was their childhood home where they spent their formative years. For Kathy and me, it was a wonderful nest where we raised our brood until they flew away one by one to explore the world on their own!

When we moved into the Lauderdale house, Sarah was about 6 and Yasmine 4. Kathy had a job as secretary to the Supreme Court Judge, Harry MacLaughlin. My office work started at 7:00 in the morning and would often extend into late evenings because of the research work that had to be done after regular clinic hours. I was also in the habit of bringing research home – you never know when good ideas might occur in your mind.

With both parents working and two young kids at home, one would think that life would be very hectic. But, it is amazing how nature has created rewards for parents in return. On the whole, children are just a bundle of love, joy and happiness – unlike anything else.

Since our marriage, I had been thinking of taking Kathy to Pakistan. I wanted her to visit the country of my birth and meet my family and relatives there. That time came in 1972. Sarah and Yasmine were old enough to be left with their grandmother. We planned our trip so that we would have time to visit a few places of interest as well, including some that I wanted to see when I was there but couldn't afford.

When we arrived at the Lahore airport, we were greeted by a number of my family members and relatives. A nephew of mine, Saifullah, drove us to Kacha Khuh in his car. There my mother and the whole clan were awaiting our arrival. I wasn't sure how my mother would react to her American daughter-in-law, but, to my amazement, Kathy was a big hit with her. Soon the word got around and a throng of neighborhood women came over to see this "pretty American lady." My mother was beaming with pride. Kathy sat down in a chair, beside my mother, and the women started asking questions. One of my nieces, Naseem, acted as the translator. These question-answer sessions were held a number of times. I teased Kathy that she was secretly relishing her "royalty status."

Kathy had brought some presents for the family. I had my sister-in-law, Bakhtawer, be the arbiter in distributing them. There were some hard feelings among a few who didn't get the presents of their choice, but Bakhtawer handled it well. The kids loved the American toys.

Our next stop was Chak 29. Most of my family and relatives had moved to Kacha Khuh, even before I came to America. Only my brother Haq and his family had stayed in Chak 29, in the house with the "big gate." Haq lived there to manage a new family farm which my parents got to own a few years after I had left for America. We visited the farm and Kathy got to pet the baby lambs. She also got to ride Haq's donkey for a photo op.

After spending a few days in Kacha Khuh and Chak 29, we came back to Lahore and stayed in the Intercontinental Hotel, located right on the famous Mall Road. We visited many of the tourist attractions in Lahore. We also did some shopping on the Mall Road and in Anarkali.

In the hotel, we were able to arrange a tour package to visit the Khyber Pass, Swat Valley, and Gilgit (a city on the Pakistani side of Kashmir). I had not been to these places before, so the tour was new to both of us.

The first leg of the trip was to fly to Peshawar. There we stayed in a hotel and got a taxi cab the next morning en route to the Khyber Pass. As we were approaching close to the area, the cab driver closed the windows and warned us about the snipers from the surrounding hills. He told us that he was not going to stop until we got to the Khyber Pass. When we got there, we looked at the narrow passage between mountains (the Hindu Kush range). A chain, hung across the pass, separated Afghanistan from Pakistan. We saw guards standing on either side of the chain, representing their respective countries. The scene looked awesome because of the historic significance of this narrow pathway between mountains – called the "Gateway to India" in the history books.

Our next destination was Swat – a beautiful valley with lush green meadows, clear lakes, and high mountains. We stayed there in a nice hotel. In the evening, the hotel guests were entertained by a local band of musicians, playing Pashto music and performing Khattack dance with swords. The whole show was very entertaining and exotic.

From Swat, we had planned to continue our trip to Chitral Valley. We had heard a lot about its beauty and grandeur. But, we had to cancel that part of the trip because too much snow in the mountains had closed up the access routes.

We came back to Rawalpindi from where our flight was supposed to depart for Gilgit. But the PIA (Pakistan International Airline) flight to Gilgit had been canceled due to bad weather. In the midst of our disappointment, the PIA somehow was able to book us on a government-sponsored commuter flight, used for transporting Kashmiri workers back and forth between Gilgit and mainland Pakistan. It was a military plane, with no frills. Fortunately, we got the window seats. Looking down the snow-capped mountains of the Karakorum Range (including K-2, the second highest mountain in the world) was worth the whole trip.

In Gilgit, we stayed in a government rest house. Although the accommodations were far from luxurious, the outside scene was spectacular. This is the place where the three mountain ranges: the Himalayas, the Karakorum, and the Hindukush – meet. The valley is surrounded by tall rugged mountains all around. It is probably the quietest place on earth.

We arranged a jeep safari into the mountains. The road had been carved out from the side of the mountains and packed with nothing more than dirt and loose rocks. With the mountain on one side and the valley floor deep on the other, there was no room for error. But the Jeep driver was quite skilled for this terrain.

In spite of the rough ride, the scenery was just spectacular. In the valley below, we could see the river with crystal clear water snaking along. We stopped for lunch at the residence of Raja of Punyal; it was part of the tour package. We did not meet the Raja, but it was great to have lunch there as his guest.

After the wonderful tour of Gigit, we flew back to Rawalpindi and then to Lahore. From Lahore, we took a train to Khanewal (a city 14 miles west of Kacha Khuh). We reserved our seats in an air conditioned coach because I had heard a lot about the amenities in these luxury coaches when I lived in Kacha Khuh in the 50's. We reserved a private compartment with attached bathroom and room service. Fine dining was available on board. We enjoyed the journey which lasted about six hours.

We spent a few more days in Kacha Khuh with my family before flying back to the US. It was great to see the kids after a long trip. They were doing well with their grandmother, although a bit spoiled because of the lavish attention they got in our absence. Sarah, in particular, had bonded with her grandma. Many years later when grandma died, Sarah went with us to Iowa and sang a song at her grandma's funeral. It was moving; it filled our eyes with tears.

Now that our two children were a bit older (Sarah was 7 and Yasmine 4), they had a number of friends they could play with on the block. We had monkey bars in the back yard where we could see them spend hours. It was a joy just to watch them. We had a good size front yard where I loved playing Itza football with them and their neighborhood friends. When the kids got on their mother's nerves, she would tell me to take them out of the house. I obeyed (I had no choice.) In the summer, parks were the place to be with the kids. In the winter, I would often take them, together with a few of their friends, to a nearby golf course. The snow covered hills of the golf course were ideal for sledding or playing our favorite game, King of the Hill.

When we lived in the Lauderdale house, we also had a boat and a trailer cabin up North, on Gull Lake in Brainerd. We would go there (about 3 hours drive from our house) on holidays and weekends. We spent some quality time together as a family.

Because Minnesota is known for its more than 10,000 lakes, fishing is a big thing in the state. After a few years, I developed a passion for it, too. I loved fishing on Gull Lake. One day, I took the kids (Sarah and Yasmine) along on the boat. As we stopped to fish, I noticed that water was leaking into the boat. I remember saying: "Girls, we are sinking." Apparently, the drain hole in the back of the boat had been left open. Yasmine found the plug but, in panic, I started the boat and drove off as fast as I could to the shore. We got to the shore, drained the boat, and plugged up the hole. From then on, the drain plug was put on the check list before any boat launch.

A few years later, we sold the trailer and bought a lakeshore lot on the Gull Lake. We built a house there. It was our summer lake home. We enjoyed it for many years to come.

In 1978, we had our third child. We named her Rachel Ann. Her first and middle name are American because, by that time, I was fully "Americanized" and didn't feel the need of inserting my ethnicity into our child's name. Nonetheless, all our kids have beautiful names. I feel there is beauty in all names as it is in all cultures.

Taking care of three young kids is a challenge for all parents but, in most cases, the lion's share of the responsibility rests with the mother. In our case, Kathy had a unique way of handling the kids if they got unruly – she was the disciplinarian. For example, on our long trips to Brainerd, the kids would sometimes get restless in the back of the van and would start fighting. What Kathy would do in that case is to pull the car over to the shoulder of the road and stop. "We are not moving unless you stop arguing," she would say. Amazingly, the tactic worked and soon we would be on our way.

A variation of Kathy's unique method of keeping discipline happened one day at the entrance of a restaurant (Lido's Café in Lauderdale). The kids started arguing with each other about something and Kathy put a stop to it by declaring that she could not take it any longer and then she left. I took the kids to the car and drove them home. They looked very concerned about where their mother had gone. I reassured them that she would be back when she had cooled off. Kids were hungry so I fixed them some eggs. After a while, Kathy showed up. The kids were happy to have their mom back. I offered eggs to Kathy but she declined. She said she had a nice pizza already. I don't know if I would recommend this method of disciplining kids to anybody else, but in our household it worked pretty well.

As the kids got older, they started losing interest in going to the lake. They would rather spend the weekends at home with their friends. In our case, also, it a long trek to Brainerd as well as the upkeep of the second home was becoming a bit tedious. So, we decided to sell the cabin. At the same time, we got interested in a home in Chanhassen (suburb of Minneapolis) which was located on a small lake (called Lotus Lake). We sold the Lauderdale home and the Gull Lake cabin to buy this house.

At the time we moved to Chanhassen, Sarah had moved out to live in an apartment. She had started her college studies at the U. Yasmine and Rachel moved with us to the Chanhassen home. After graduating from Roseville High School, Yasmine enrolled at the U and moved out to live in her apartment by herself and with Blaze, her cat. Rachel was nine when we moved to Chanhassen. She transferred from Roseville Elementary to Clear Springs Elementary School (not far from our house).

We stayed in the Chanhassen home for about 7 years. It was a big house with an indoor swimming pool, Jacuzzi, sauna, and a hot tub in the master bedroom. All these amenities offered a resort-like living that we enjoyed immensely.

The Chanhassen house was great but it required a lot of upkeep, like keeping the pool clean and maintaining its chemistry. Also, we had a boat but the dock slip belonged to the neighborhood association and was available only during part of the boating season. So, we started looking for a lakeshore homes on Lake Minnetonka. In 1994, we found one in Orono (our present home) that met our needs perfectly. It is a rambler, located on one of the bays (called North Arm Bay) of Lake Minnetonka. We have a lakeshore, a canopied dock for the boat, and gorgeous views of the lake from every room. So far as I am concerned, it couldn't get better than that!

Rachel stayed with us in Orono until she graduated from Minnetonka High School and went to Hamline University in St. Paul. She stayed in a rooming house near the campus until she graduated with a Bachelor of Science degree. At this time, we were both working; Kathy at the Supreme Court as secretary to Judge Rosalie Wahl and I as Professor and Director of Radiation Physics Section in the Department of Radiation Oncology at the University Hospital.

Now that the kids were gone and engaged in their educational and professional careers, Kathy and I entered a new phase in life – the life of empty nesters. Actually, it is not a bad life as long as I don't get in Kathy's hair like the kids used to.

Friends in Lahore. From left to right: Me, Shaukat, and Naqvi ,1963

Mom (1972)

Rab and his family - 1972

Bakhtawar, Sardar, Zuhra, and Kids - 1972

Haq and his family - 1972

Shah and his family - 1972

Z.A. and his daughter Zakia - 1972

Satar and his family - 1972

Dost and his family - 1972

Kathy in Chak 29 - 1972

Return to Chak 29 - 2000

Door to my childhood home - 2000

My High School Kacha Khuh - 2000

Reception for my family by students of my nephew Kamran's school in Kacha Khuh - 2000

Photo with my family in Pakistan - 2000

Rachel, Kathy, and Sarah in Pakistan - 2000

From Left to right: Z.A.'s grandson Adnan, Rachel, Sarah, and Yasmine - 2000

Taj Mahal - 2000

Sarah with maternal grandparents - 1967

Our family in Lauderdale - 1980

Our three daughters, Kathy and her family - 1979

Sarah with her dog - 2017

Yasmine - 2017

Rachel - 2017

Kathy and me - 2017

Chapter 11

Professional Career and Service

My professional career began in 1960 when I was hired as the first medical physicist in Pakistan. Until then I had not heard of physicists working in the medical field. So, let me say that I had not planned on going into medical physics – I just stumbled into it.

In 1963 as a Fulbright Scholar, America gave me the opportunity to further my studies. I got my doctorate degree in biophysics in 1969, which allowed me to advance my career in medical physics. It is said that America is a land of opportunity. In my case, it turned out to be a whale of an opportunity. Now it was all up to me to make the best of it.

My background in physics, math, and biology equipped me very well to pursue my interest in teaching, research, and clinical work as a medical physicist. Being a non-physician, I had to carve out a role for myself to work with the physicians and other medical staff. I had read a book by a famous radiotherapist (radiation oncologist), Dr. Ralston Paterson, where he stated: "In radiotherapy the physicist who has given special study to this field is full partner with the therapist, not only in the development of the science, but in the day-to-day treatment of patients. The unit team, therefore, even for the smallest department, consists of a radiotherapist and a physicist."[1] That statement has been my guide throughout my career.

In the U.S., I started working in the radiation therapy department of the University of Minnesota Hospitals in 1965, as a teaching assistant. I got my on-the-job clinical training from Dr. Vaughn Moore, who was the Chief Medical Physicist at that time. He had certification from the American Board of Radiology (ABR) in radiological physics. So, he met the requirements of a "qualified medical physicist," as currently defined by the American Association of Physicists in Medicine (AAPM). I was lucky to have a qualified medical physicist, Dr. Moore, supervise my clinical training.

Right after receiving my doctorate degree in 1969, I was appointed Assistant Professor. My responsibilities included clinical physics service, teaching, and research. In the clinic, my main job was to calibrate and check the accuracy of radiation therapy machines and plan radiation treatments for individual patients. In addition, it was expected of me to provide consultation to the radiation oncologists regarding optimal use of radiation treatments, and design and maintain a radiation protection program for patients and personnel.

In 1974, I was promoted to the position of Associate Professor with tenure. The same year, I obtained my ABR board-certification in therapeutic radiological physics. Shortly after that, Dr. Moore left the department and moved to another institution in North Dakota. To fill his position, I was appointed the Director of the Radiation Physics Section. I retained that position until my retirement in 2001.

In the early days when I started my career, medical physicists in most institutions were relegated primarily to the job of equipment maintenance, calibration, and radiation dosage calculations. Their input to the treatment planning process was limited or non-existent. In other words, they were not a "full partner" with the radiation therapist as Dr. Paterson had

---

[1] Ralston Paterson, *The Treatment of Malignant Disease by Radiotherapy*, 2nd ed. (Baltimore: Williams & Wilkins, 1963: 527).

emphasized in his book. I realized the importance of medical physics input to the whole treatment planning process. I teamed up with Dr. Levitt, our department Chairman, to build up the needed collaboration between medical physicists and radiation oncologists in the planning of patient treatments. We designed a system in which each patient was to have an assigned medical physicist who would assist the physician in formulating the best possible treatment plan. We also made a requirement that both the medical physicist and the physician would have to approve the final treatment plan. And subsequently, both would have to oversee proper implementation of the plan.

In an academic institution like ours, medical physicists participate in teaching and training of radiation oncology residents, graduate students, dosimetrists, and therapists. In my lectures and personal interaction, my mission was to make complex physics concepts understandable to this audience of varied backgrounds. As a teacher, my reward was not only to have the residents and other professionals pass the physics part of their specialty board exams but also be fully conversant with the application of physics in their professional practice.

In a busy department, clinical service and teaching responsibilities leave very little time for research. In my case, I also had administrative responsibilities as director of the medical physics section. That made it all the more difficult to find time for research during regular working hours. But I loved research. Accordingly, I gave research no less priority than my teaching and clinical service responsibilities. I didn't mind working late in the evenings and on weekends. Research was important to me not only for my professional advancement but also my intellectual needs as a physicist.

In 1979, my academic record, including research publications, teaching, and clinical service, was reviewed by the University Tenure and Promotions Committee. On the basis of that review, I was promoted to full professorship. Not only was it a great honor for me, it provided me an incentive to continue my endeavor towards further advancement of my professional career.

Because of my research publications and paper presentations at national meetings, I had attained a modest degree of name recognition among my peers. One day (in 1978 I believe), an agent from a publishing company dropped by in my office. After introducing herself, she told me that she had been referred to me by someone who thought I might be interested in writing a textbook on medical physics. I was pleasantly surprised and, without hesitation, answered in the affirmative. She asked me to write up a book proposal and, with a sample chapter, send it to the Editor of Williams & Wilkins in Baltimore, MD.

In the book proposal that I sent to the publisher, I expressed my desire to write a book for the radiation therapy team that included radiation oncologists, medical physicists, dosimetrists, and radiotherapy technologists. This was to be achieved by maintaining a careful balance between theory and practical details.

After a few weeks, the publisher sent me the comments of their technical reviewers. They were all favorable except the comment of one of the reviewers who maintained that no one could write a textbook for such an audience of mixed educational backgrounds. In other words, you could write a book for each specialty individually but not one book that would meet the needs of all members of the radiation therapy team. I answered back to the publisher saying that a conscious effort would be made to make the subject palatable to those not formally trained in physics but at the same time not to diminish the value of the book to the medical physicists. The publisher agreed and accepted my proposal.

It took me about 5 years to write the book. I titled it: *The Physics of Radiation Therapy*. It was published in 1984. To my great amazement, the book became the best seller in the field of radiation therapy physics. Because of its popularity, the publisher asked me to continue updating the book on a regular basis to keep up with the advancements in the field. Accordingly, I published the second edition in 1993, the third in 2003, the fourth in 2010, and the fifth (the current edition) in 2014.

In parallel with the physics textbook, I thought I should also work on another title that would be specifically dedicated to treatment planning. Since treatment planning in radiation oncology encompasses both the physics and clinical aspects, I asked one of my physician colleagues, Dr. Roger Potish, to co-edit the book with me. Together, we invited prominent radiation oncologists, medical physicists, and radiation biologists to contribute articles for the book. The first edition, titled: *Treatment Planning in Radiation Oncology*, was published in 1998 by Williams and Wilkins.

In 2005, my dear friend Roger passed away. It hit me hard. I had worked with him for 35 years. I will always remember him as a great physician and an esteemed colleague. When the publisher asked me to consider the second edition of *Treatment Planning in Radiation Oncology*, I decided to work on it as a solo editor. I dedicated the second edition in memoriam to Dr. Roger A. Potish (1947 – 2005). It was published in 2007. Subsequently, I co-edited the third edition with Dr. Bruce Gerbi (medical physicist) and the fourth edition with Dr. John Gibbons (medical physicist) and Dr. Paul Sperdutto (radiation oncologist). These editions were published in 2012 and 2016, respectively.

During my tenure at the U, I had taken an active interest in the professional organizations, especially the AAPM. I volunteered my services to work on various scientific and professional committees. For several years, I served on the certification boards, the ABR and the ABMP (American Board of Medical Physics). In 1989, I was elected President of the AAPM.

The most important thing I did as the AAPM president was to appoint a presidential ad hoc committee to study the feasibility of clinical residency training for medical physicists. Prior to that time, medical physicists got their training on the job. Board certification was available but that did not assure that the candidates had sufficient clinical training before taking the exam. Consequently, there was no assurance that a medical physicist working in the clinical environment was fully trained and qualified. That posed serious risk to patients.

I attended every meeting of the ad hoc committee to provide my input. After a few months, the committee came up with the recommendation that medical physicists must go through structured clinical training, just like the physician residents, before taking their board certification exam. The committee report was approved by the AAPM and published in 1989. Subsequently, several institutions have adopted the report as a template for their physics residency training programs. Currently, the ABR will not certify unless the candidate has successfully completed an accredited residency program. I feel a sense of pride in that I was instrumental in creating a nation-wide program that has put medical physicists on a par with the physicians in terms of their qualifications to provide vital services in the clinic.

In 1999, I was awarded the William D. Coolidge Gold Medal by the AAPM. According to the AAPM, "This award recognizes an AAPM member for an eminent career in medical physics. It is the highest award given by the AAPM."

Receiving the Coolidge Award was a great honor but it also got me thinking that maybe it was time for me to retire. After a long and productive career in my estimation, I was ready to hang up my hat. So, I retired from the U as Professor Emeritus in January, 2001.

Just before retirement, I took my family to visit Pakistan. I wanted my kids to see the places where I was born and raised. My mother had passed away by that time, but I wanted my American family to meet my Pakistani family before I would be gone, too.

In Lahore, we stayed with my brother Z.A. and his daughter Zakia. My brother was not in the best of health at that time and was a bit fragile but his sense of humor was as good as ever. We enjoyed laughing about old jokes. With Zakia as our guide, we visited many places of interest in Lahore, including Government College, Mall road, Anarkali bazaar, Jinnah Gardens, Shalimar Gardens, and Lahore Fort. Traffic in Lahore is absolutely hectic, but Zakia showed us her driving skills when we rode with her in her car.

We took a bus to Kacha Khuh. As we arrived there and came off the bus, we were greeted by my brothers and nephews. Soon, a question came up about where we would be staying: would it be with my brother Shah or my nephew Saifullah? It was a hard decision. I did not want to hurt anyone's feelings. Finally, I decided to stay with Saifullah because his house was big enough to accommodate us and had amenities that better suited my American family. Later, I learned that it did not sit well with my brother. From my end though, it was just a misunderstanding. Staying with Saifullah was not indicative of my lesser respect or love for Shah. I loved him very much, as I did all my brothers and sisters!

We spent a few days in Kacha Khuh to meet my family including nephews and nieces and their offspring. We had a wonderful time. After that, we visited Multan and had a brief tour of the city, including my old alma mater, Emerson College. It brought back old memories. We also dropped by the house of my nephew Sher Dil and his family in Khanewal. Sher Dil is the son of my oldest sister, Sardar, who had passed away before we visited Pakistan. Sher has engineering degree and some in the family addressed him as Engineer. When we visited him, he was retired from engineering profession but was thriving as a business man.

Of course, we couldn't miss going to Chak 29. As we arrived there, a crowd of people gathered around us. One person approached me and introduced himself. I had no problem recognizing him, in spite of his white beard. He was my cousin (son of my aunt). Apparently, he still lived in Chak 29. After a hug, we had a brief family chat.

As I looked around, the streets and the village square didn't resemble the image I had of it in my mind. The only structure I could recognize was the mosque with tall minarets. Then we went to see my old house with the gate. It was still there but none of my family members lived there anymore. When I looked at the gate, it appeared much smaller than what I had in my memories. My kids' explanation made sense: When I was a boy, the gate looked bigger than it looked now. I did recognize the ring on the gate that I used to play with. So, it must be the same old gate.

Nothing much remained of my elementary school. That beautiful brick building with brick-paved verandas was no longer there. The whole building was in ruins, deserted, and taken over by sand. It made me feel sad.

After spending a couple of weeks in Pakistan, we flew to India, to see the Taj Mahal. The Taj is located in the city of Agra, about 120 miles from New Delhi. I had arranged a limo to pick us up at the New Delhi airport and drive us to the hotel in Agra where we had arranged to stay for a couple days. The traffic in the city was nothing less than a chaos. You could see cars, busses, rickshaws, scooters, and trucks honking and zigzagging their way through the crazy traffic. Once in awhile, we would come across cows roaming free on the road. Being an animal lover, I didn't mind it at all. They looked so cute!

The Taj Mahal (meaning Crown of the Palace) is a breathtaking piece of architecture. It is a mausoleum built in 1632 by the Mughal emperor, Shah Jahan, to house the tomb of his wife, Mumtaz Mahal. Shortly after completion of the Taj Mahal, Shah Jahan was deposed by his son, Aurangzeb, and was kept under house arrest until his death. He is buried in the mausoleum, next to his wife.

It took us a day to tour the Taj Mahal complex. We stayed in the palace compound until dusk to observe the glow of its ivory-white marble. It looked magnificent in the moonlight. No wonder, it has been designated as one of the Seven Wonders of the World.

The trip to Pakistan with my family was my last one. Since then lots of things have happened worldwide that have taken the pleasure out of travelling abroad. I wait for the day when the scourge of terrorism is wiped out from the face of the earth and people will be able to travel freely like it used to be before September 11, 2001.

After retiring in January, 2001, I continued some of my professional activities as Professor Emeritus. The department had asked me to give a few lectures each semester and mentor graduate students. That was great because it allowed me to stay involved in academic activities while enjoying the fruits of my retirement. At home, I spend most of my new-found free time in going regularly to the gym every morning and reading and writing the rest of the day.

During 35 years of my active career and 10 years of post retirement, I have visited about 35 countries. The majority of these trips were in conjunction with workshops organized by Professor Azam Noorimandrad of George Washington University and sponsored by the AAPM and the IOMP (International Organization of Medical Physics). Besides professional service, the best thing about these workshops was that my wife accompanied me on these trips. We planned the trips so that after the workshops, we could spend some time sightseeing and visiting places of interest. Often, we took side trips with the other faculty members. Some of the greatest times we had on these trips were with a select group of American faculty (and their spouses): Jim and Marilyn, Bhudatt and Michelle, and Ted and Shar. In acknowledgement, many thanks to Azam and the sponsoring organizations for facilitating these educational trips!

Chapter 12

Quest for Ultimate Reality

The best thing about retirement is the freedom from the daily routine of going to the office, spending all day at work, and thinking at night about what you did and what you would be doing the next day. My job was extra stressful because it involved tasks that could critically impact patient care. There was simply no room for error. In spite of the fact that I had a great job as a tenured professor and director of medical physics section, I started to entertain the thought of retiring a few years early because of the stressful nature of my job. Accordingly, I retired in January 2001, at the age of sixty two.

Retirement is indeed a new phase in one's life. In my case, it took a few months to settle down in my daily activities such as a morning walk or a workout at the gym, preparing for lectures at the U that I had been contracted to give each semester, and writing updates for my two textbooks. In spite of these not too hard activities, I had plenty of time on hands to do things I liked most doing, namely, reading the daily newspaper and sundry books and magazines of general interest. Once in a while I would mull over questions of existential nature such as the creation of our universe, its evolution, and its destiny.

During my formal education in physics, I had not taken any courses directly related to astronomy or astrophysics. But once I retired, I had plenty of free time to read books and articles on cosmology – the science of cosmic origin and its evolution. The more I read about cosmology, the more I got intrigued by the proposition: Did God create the universe or did it appear by itself? It was a strange proposition, though, because I had never questioned God's existence before. But after a superficial reading of the Big Bang theory of the universe, I began to reframe the God question this way: Do the laws of physics allow spontaneous creation of our universe? If not, then there must be a power outside the laws of physics that created the universe. But if the laws of physics were not violated at the Big Bang, then there is no need to hypothesize an outside agent responsible for creating the universe.

An in-depth study of the Big Bang theory convinced me that the laws of physics as we know them did indeed allow the creation of our universe by itself. In other words, it is not necessary for us to assume that some extraneous agent must have created the universe. There is a strong scientific evidence that at the instant of the Big Bang conditions existed that could have created the universe from nothing.

A vast amount of scientific literature exists on the creation and evolution of our universe. In my case, the following books were most helpful: *The Fabric of the Cosmos*, by Brian Greene; *A Brief History of Time*, by Stephen Hawking; *The God Particle*, by Leon Lederman; and *Nothingness*, by Henning Genz. Of course, the public libraries and the Internet were a great reservoir of knowledge from which I extensively drew upon to understand the under-pinning of the Big Bang theory. Also, having a formal education in physics, math, and biology, allowed me to delve more deeply into the science of creation than an average lay-person would. More importantly, it helped me examine the credibility of a scientific theory that I read in the literature.

I broadened my study of cosmology to include the beginning of the universe, cosmic evolution, and biologic evolution. My plan was to eventually contrast the scientific view of creation with the creationist view held by the world's major religions. After researching into the scientific and religious realms for several years, I felt elated by the knowledge I had gained in the process; so much so that I started entertaining the thought of writing a book. I wanted to share the insight I had gained with others. After five years of researching and writing, I was able to publish the book, *Our Universe: A Scientific and Religious View of Creation*, in 2007.

Writing a book is a great experience. One thing I had learned from my previous writings was the fact that you cannot get an idea across to readers unless you understand it yourself. But even if you understand it well, it is not always easy to express it in words that would be understandable to readers of varied background and education. The book I wrote about the universe had an additional difficulty. It involved complex scientific concepts that are hard to explain in lay-persons' terms. Admittedly, in the case of the first part of the book where I discuss the scientific theory of creation, my wife commented that it read like a textbook.

Hoping to avoid another textbook style of writing, I will include in this chapter only a brief story of my quest for an answer to a fundamental question at the very core of our existence – How the universe came into being? Here it goes.

Once upon a time, there was no time, no space, no matter, no nothing. This is the moment (at time zero) when the Big Bang occurred – about 13.7 billion years ago. The instant of the Big Bang has been arrived at by extrapolating the observed expansion of the universe (which is still expanding today) to its beginning. This is like playing the cosmic movie backward to its starting point.

At the starting point, you can imagine the universe to be a teeny-tiny (infinitesimal) speck. But the speck was packed with the entire energy of the universe (equivalent to all the matter and energy of the current universe). This is the moment of the Big Bang – the moment when space, time, and the entire energy content of the universe came into existence. Nothing existed before the Big Bang.

The question arises as to what gave rise to the Big Bang. After extensive study of the cosmology literature, I have yet to find a clear-cut answer that I could give here in a layperson's terms. Nonetheless, stating in physics terms, the Big Bang was the result of quantum fluctuations of energy density, as characterized by Werner Heisenberg's uncertainty principle. In other words, the universe came into existence spontaneously in accordance with the natural laws of quantum mechanics. There is no need to assume prior causation or a prime mover.

A more poetic description of the likely birth scene of our universe is provided by Leon Lederman, a Nobel Laureate in physics, in his book, *The God Particle*:

> In the beginning there was void—a curious form of vacuum—a nothingness containing no space, no time, no matter, no light, no sound....The curious vacuum held potential. Then the nothingness exploded...Out of this energy, matter emerged—dense plasma of particles that dissolved into radiation and back to matter. Particles collided and gave birth to new particles. Space and time boiled and formed as black holes formed and dissolved. What a scene![2]

Space and time came into existence at the Big Bang and the universe started expanding immediately at an exorbitant speed – much faster than the speed of light. This initial inflationary growth spurt was critical for the survival of the baby universe because it allowed the universe to escape the enormous gravity (close to infinity) which could have crushed the embryonic universe. Thank you inflation!

There are other scientific theories of how our universe came into existence. But they are variations of the one basic theme, namely, that the universe sprang out of nothing. This prompted Alan Guth, the father of the inflation

---

[2] Leon Lederman, *The God Particle* (Boston, New York: Houghton Mifflin Company, 1993).

theory, to comment: "It's often said there is no such thing as a free lunch. But the universe itself may be a free lunch."

Coming back to the original proposition: Did the laws of physics allow spontaneous creation of the universe? After extensive research into the scientific literature, I would say yes. Stephen Hawking stated it more emphatically in his book, *The Grand Design*:

> … the beginning of the universe was governed by the laws of science and does not need to be set in motion by some god.[3]

The beginning of the universe by itself elicits some difficult questions. For instance: What happened before the Big Bang? What existed before the Big Bang? Where did the laws of physics come from? Literature is rife with all kinds of answers, some serious and some speculative. Let me add a few of my own.

With regard to the first two questions, it is credible to believe that nothing happened or existed before the Big Bang because time and space simply did not exist prior to that moment. The third question falls more in the realm of metaphysics than physics. It may be logical to assume that the laws of physics are the properties of the universe that came into play at its beginning and would continue to govern it as long as it exists. Humans, being themselves the product of the universe, have evolved to develop cognitive faculties including consciousness, perception and thinking. They have the ability to study the laws of nature and use them to explain natural phenomena. If the above answer is slipping into the metaphysical realm, let me offer another one in the form of a question: Which came first, the Big Bang or the laws of physics? You will have the right answer when you figure out whether the chicken came first or the egg!

My quest for the ultimate reality also included my desire to find answer to another fundamental question: What is my origin as a human being? I was

---

[3] Stephen Hawking and Leonard Milodinow, *The Grand Design* (New York: Bantam Books, 2010), 135.

familiar with the story of Adam and Eve but without scientific evidence the ancient story just didn't cut it. There must be a more logical explanation. Fortunately, the scientific literature on human evolution is abundant, including the famous book, *On the Origin of Species by Means of Natural Selection*, by British naturalist Charles Darwin. The conclusion I reached after researching the literature are stated in my book, *Our Universe.* An excerpt summarizes it as below:

> There is strong scientific evidence that human beings evolved on Earth from the first cells of life, called prokaryotes, some three billion years ago. These single-celled organisms were the result of atomic and molecular interactions on the surface of the earth under the right chemical and environmental conditions. There is no doubt that the first life was created by the same laws of physics and chemistry as those that govern the nonliving things. There is no evidence of an 'intelligent designer' of life.[4]

The theory that species have descended from a common ancestor – the progenitor organism – is supported by the fact that all living organisms use the same genetic material, amino acids, proteins, and cell-division process for their reproduction and metabolism. The universality of these traits at the molecular and functional level strongly suggests their common descent.

The idea that the initial conditions on earth created the organic molecules that are the building blocks of life has been tested in the laboratory. In 1953, Stanley Miller, of the University Chicago, conducted experiments to simulate conditions that might have produced complex organic molecules on the early earth. He subjected a gaseous mixture of hydrogen, ammonia, and methane (molecules thought to be present in the early earth's atmosphere about 3 billion years ago) in a vessel containing water to electrical sparks for several days. At the end of the experiment, he found a reddish brown residue rich in amino acids.

---

[4] Faiz M. Khan, *Our Universe: A Scientific and Religious View of Creation* (Bloomington, Indiana: iUniverse, 2007), 178.

Since Miller's experiment, scientists have been able to produce all twenty of the amino acids as well as purine and pyrimidine bases, the building blocks of nucleic acids like the RNA and the DNA and a number of other molecules essential to life. Also, there have been several reports of scientists creating life in the lab through abiogenesis – a process of generating living organisms from lifeless matter. For example, in 2010, living cells powered by man-made DNA were produced at the J. Craig Venter Institute. The old myth that life on earth was deliberately created by an intelligent designer has been thoroughly debunked.

The understanding of human origin is derived largely from the analysis of fossil records, geological history, large-scale migration of species, genetics, and the Darwinian theory of natural selection. Based on these carefully collected and analyzed data, the scientists have classified human beings as part of the Linnaean taxonomy classification system. Although human evolution goes back to the very origin of life on earth, modern humans belong to the Kingdom *Animalia*, Order *Primates*, Genus *Homo*, and Species *Sapiens.*

In the words of Stephen Hawking: "We are just an advanced breed of monkeys on a minor planet of a very average star. But we can understand the Universe. That makes us very special."[5]

[5] Stephen Hawking, *Der Spiegel* (17 October 1988).

Chapter 13

Road to Enlightenment

My quest for the ultimate reality revealed certain fundamental truths. The following excerpt from page 176 of my book, *Our Universe*[6], talks about the process I went through before I felt I was truly enlightened.

> After a long and arduous search for truth, I feel enlightened about what I have learned about the universe, God, religion, and humanist philosophies. I feel that anyone can undertake such a journey and thus get rewarded. The only precondition is that the seeker of truth must cast aside prejudices as much as humanly possible. It is the prejudice that kills the chances of finding the truth. Once you break out of your inherited beliefs and prejudices, you are intellectually free. With a free mind, you can acquire new wisdoms and untainted understandings of things from the great reservoir of human knowledge that exists today.

[6] Faiz M. Khan, *Our Universe: A scientific and Religious View of Creation* (Bloomington, Indiana: iUniverse, 2007).

Enlightenment allowed me to obtain objective truth about many things such as the origin of the universe, evolution of life, and religions. Most importantly, enlightenment gave me the courage to free myself from superstition and other unsubstantiated beliefs prevalent in most cultures and societies. After casting away the yoke of irrational traditionalism through scientific reason, I can now rely on my own intellectual capacity in determining what is credible and what is not. In a sense, I am self-directed in thought and action. I am elated by this feeling of self-empowerment.

In the final chapter of the book, *Our Universe*, I listed my principles of enlightenment and called them the guiding principles of my life. But, I also encouraged my readers to "utilize their own creative minds in the fulfillment of their goals in life." After all, enlightenment is attainable only through awakening one's own intellectual power of reason.

I must admit that on my road to enlightenment, religion posed the greatest challenge. It demanded blind faith in the supernatural. Most people learn about God from their parents, friends, preachers, and scriptures. Scriptures present a powerful testimony to God's existence but it is based on divine revelation or inspiration received by men in the ancient past. We cannot cross-examine the authors of these scriptures. Stories are beautiful to read but there is no denying the fact that they all appeal to our emotions and belief in the unknown.

I was raised a Muslim but I had exposure to other religions as well. When I came to the U.S., I had a chance to socialize with American and international students of different faiths and cultures. On occasions, I had encounters with the evangelical Christians called Campus Crusaders. I remember chatting frequently with one of the evangelists about the teachings of Christ and Muhammad. Once we debated about whether Jesus Christ was the Son of God or a Prophet as the Muslims believe. These conversations were quite cordial but never reached a point of either one of us conceding to the other's point of view.

Like most people, I took my religion for granted most of my life, never questioning my beliefs. But all that changed when I undertook the study of major religions in order to answer the question: Did God create life, or did the world appear spontaneously? At the end of extensive reading and soul-searching, I was able to answer that question in *Our Universe.*

Although my study of religions focused primarily on the creation of the universe, I kept my eyes open on the moral foundations laid out in the scriptures. On the whole, I found scriptural messages and injunctions to be socially beneficial. However, there were some that could be interpreted as contradictory to God's attribute of being Merciful and Just. Let me point out a few examples.

As told in the Bible (and corroborated by the Qur'an), God destroyed the cities of Sodom and Gomorrah with "brimstone and fire from the LORD out of heaven." (Gen. 19:24–26)[7]. If "God so loved the world" (John 3:16), then how could He have drowned the whole planet (Noah's flood) as described below?

> And every living substance was destroyed which was upon the face of the ground, both man and cattle, and the creeping things, and the fowl of the heaven.
>
> (Gen. 7:23)

And God's punishment for nonbelievers:

> And the smoke of their torment ascendeth up for ever and ever: and they have no rest day nor night, who worship the beast and his image, and whosoever receiveth the mark of his name.
>
> (Revelation 14:11)

> Truly Hell is as a place of ambush,
> For the transgressors a place of destination:
> They will dwell therein for ages.
> Nothing cool shall they taste therein, nor any drink,

[7] *Holy Bible* (Nashville, Tennesee: King James Version; Regency Publishing House, 1971).

> Save a boiling fluid and a fluid, dark,
> Murky, intensely cold,
> A fitting recompense (for them).
>
> (Surah 78:21–26)[8]

From these and the other verses in the Scriptures, it becomes apparent that God's love, mercy, and kindness are reserved for the faithful. For the nonbelievers and sinful, there is nothing but a place in hell wherein to burn for eternity.

Admittedly, the concept of heaven and hell is based on reward and punishment. But one cannot ignore the fact that the description of hell in the scriptures exceeds the human standards of punishment for any crime, no matter how grievous. Even the United States Constitution (Amendment VIII) prohibits the government from inflicting cruel and unusual punishment in criminal prosecutions.

Another problem we see in the scriptures concerns the status of women. Shouldn't all men and women be equal in the eyes of the Lord? Apparently that is not the case according to the following verses in the scriptures of the three major religions of the world:

> In childhood, a female must be subject to her father, in youth to her husband, when her lord is dead, to her sons; a woman must never be independent.
>
> (Laws of Manu 5:148)[9]

> Wives, submit yourselves unto your husbands, as unto the Lord. For the husband is the head of the wife, even as Christ is the head of the church: and he is the savior of the body. Therefore as the church is subject unto Christ, so let the wives be to their husbands in everything.
>
> (Eph. 5:22–24)

---

[8] *The Qur'an* (Elmhurst, New York: Translated by Abdullah Yusuf Ali; Tahrike Tarsile Qur'an, Inc. Publishers, 1999).

[9] http://www.sacred-texts.com/hin/manu/manu05.htm

> Men are the protectors and maintainers of women, because Allah has given the one more (strength) than the other, and because they support them from their means. Therefore the righteous women are devoutly obedient, and guard in (the husband's) absence what Allah would have them guard. As to those women on whose part you fear disloyalty and ill-conduct, admonish them (first), (next), refuse to share their beds, (and last), beat them (lightly); but if they return to obedience, do not seek against them means (of annoyance): for Allah is Most High, Great (above you all).
>
> (Surah 4:34–35)

How about slavery? It is simply mind-boggling that God, the Creator of all beings, did not explicitly forbid the inhuman practice of slavery. He, in fact, condoned it in the Old Testament as well as the New Testament. Let us take a look:

> If a man smite his servant, or his maid with a rod, and he die under his hand; he shall be surely punished. Notwithstanding, if he continues a day or two, he shall not be punished.
>
> (Exod. 21:20–21)

> Then you shall take an awl, and thrust it through his ear unto the door, and he shall be thy servant forever. And also unto thy maidservant you shall do likewise.
>
> (Deut. 15:17)

Jesus was asked to visit and heal a slave who was sick. Jesus did not say anything to free the slave. Instead he complimented the slave owner for his faith:

> I say unto you, I have not found so great faith, no, not in Israel.
>
> (Luke 7:9)

Regarding the duties of slaves, the Bible says:

> Servants, be obedient to them that are your masters according to the flesh, with fear and trembling, in singleness of your heart, as unto Christ.
>
> (Eph. 6:5)

The Qur'an did not ban slavery outright as it banned pig's meat, alcohol, idolatry, and many other ungodly customs and rituals. However, it did promote the freeing of slaves. Here is a sample:

> It is not righteousness that you turn your faces toward East or West, but it is righteousness…to spend of your substance…for the ransom of slaves.
>
> (Surah 2:177)

> Verily we have created Man into toil and struggle…And what will explain to you the path that is steep? (It is) freeing the bondman.
>
> (Surah 90:4–13)

In spite of some apparent glitches, if taken literally, scriptures are beautiful pieces of literature to read and draw moral lessons from. Let me end this commentary on scriptures with the following excerpt from page 174 of *Our Universe.*

> Historically, religions have been in the forefront of bringing morality into the world. Prophets and scriptures brought light into the dark ages of human civilization. Through morality, man was transformed from being a savage animal to a civilized human being. However, we have come a long way from the era of prophets and scriptures. This is the age of science. We should guide ourselves through scientific reasoning while respecting our roots and each other's faith, whatever that may be. This is the age of enlightenment.

For me, religion is a personal matter. All humans have the fundamental right of choosing and following their own spiritual, religious, or secular path in life. However, religious exclusivity and literal conformity to the scriptural doctrines give rise to fundamentalism which does not bode well for either the religions or the people they serve. Imposing religious dogma on others and demanding loyalty to it is tantamount to taking away their right to freedom of thought and reason.

My journey towards enlightenment led me to adopt a social philosophy called humanism. It is an ethical system that affirms nature, dignity, and ability of a person to determine his/her moral and ethical conduct without recourse to supernaturalism. Basic principles of humanism are contained in the Humanist Manifesto by the American Humanist Association. The most current manifesto, *Manifesto III*[10], lists the following primary themes:

1. Knowledge of the world is derived by observation, experimentation, and rational analysis.
2. Humans are an integral part of nature, the result of evolutionary change, an unguided process.
3. Ethical values are derived from human need and interest as tested by experience.
4. Life's fulfillment emerges from individual participation in the service of humane ideals.
5. Humans are social by nature and find meaning in relationships.
6. Working to benefit society maximizes individual happiness.

I end this chapter with the cartoon comments of L. K. Hanson in the Opinion Exchange page of *Star Tribune*, March 5, 2018:

> I don't believe in an afterlife, so I don't have to spend my whole life fearing hell, or fearing heaven even more. For whatever the tortures of hell, I think the boredom of heaven would be even worse." (Isaac Asimov (1920 – 1992))

[10] https://americanhumanist.org/what-is-humanism/manifesto3/

Chapter 14

Going Vegetarian

I became vegetarian at the ripe old age of seventy-one (It is never too late to make the conversion!). My decision to stop eating meat was not made in some sudden fit of sentimentality. I mulled over the idea for years. The serious soul-searching, however, began on a day when I had to clean a live fish that I had caught. It was such a heart-wrenching experience for me that I could not get it out of my mind. The anguish and guilt that I felt was so great that I began to link meat-eating with animal killing. It was guilt by association.

Initially the guilt feeling was only slight—lessened somewhat by excuses like "the animal is already dead" or "the meat is already prepared, so my eating it would not save the animal." But the feelings of guilt gradually grew stronger and reached a point when I could no longer hide behind my flimsy excuses. I seriously began to entertain the thought of converting to vegetarianism. The story of the doomed fish narrated below describes the state of my mind when I was finally ready to free myself from the guilt of being a carnivore.

One late afternoon, about 20 years ago, I was fishing off my lake-home dock. Suddenly I saw the fish line jiggle. When I pulled up the line, I saw a huge fish jump in the air. My heart started pounding with excitement.

The fish was bigger than I was used to catching. I started reeling it in but the fish resisted with all its might. For a moment I thought I was going to lose the battle as my fishing rod was bent almost to its breaking point. After a few minutes of struggle, the fish began to ease up, although very grudgingly. I brought it close enough to gently coax it into the net. It was a large-mouth bass—my favorite. I took out the pliers to remove the hook which had lodged deep in its throat. After some struggle, I was able to extract it. The fish was twisting and convulsing during all this time as if to make a last ditch effort to get free. Maybe it was feeling excruciating pain from the ravages of the hook and its bloody extraction.

I quickly strung in a rope through the fish's large mouth and one of its gills. I tied the rope to the dock post and threw the fish back in the lake. I watched it swim around aimlessly in the water, although restrained by the rope in every direction. While it was still making futile attempts to escape, I was assessing the ill effects of the hook and my slipshod surgery to extract it. For some reason, that day I was looking at the fish as an animal that was capable of feeling pain just like me. Never before had I felt such a concern for a fish before. Maybe I had mellowed with age and had started to feel more compassion about living things in general – animals, birds, and even insects if they were of the harmless kind. I had even felt uneasy in stringing the worm on the hook that day.

After watching the fish struggle for a while, a question popped up in my mind: Do fish feel pain? I had heard it from several fishermen that the fish do not feel pain when hooked in the mouth—it is just a cartilage, they said, devoid of any nerves or sensation. I was skeptical of the science behind this assertion but had never taken the time to check it out. I was content with my thrill of fishing. I had no concern for the fish's suffering. The thought of fish feeling the pain had never crossed my mind. And even if it did, it would be a fleeting one.

Although I was always nuts about fishing, I was not too fond of cleaning the fish. It is quite a messy process. I remember once taking my fish to a cleaning house at a lake resort where other fishermen were cleaning theirs. I was a bit shaken to watch a guy bashing the head of a large Northern.

When I asked another person why he was doing that, I was told that a quick blow on the fish's head knocks it out of its senses and consequently keeps it from struggling during the cleaning process. After seeing a few of the fish heads being smashed, I decided not to clean my fish in that atmosphere of violence. I brought the fish back to my cabin. Then someone, probably my wife, suggested that I should put the fish in the fridge overnight and clean it the next day. The idea appealed to me. At least I didn't have to bash the head of the poor thing.

The fridge idea seemed more "antiseptic" to me. The thought, however, did not cross my mind that it is probably just as painful, if not more so, for the fish to be in the fridge without oxygen and freeze to death than it would be with a blow on its head. Nonetheless, after the fridge treatment, I had no trouble cleaning the fish. The fish was already dead and did not struggle a bit during cleaning. More importantly, it did not stir my feelings for the fish.

Coming back to the story of my fish that I had left in the lake overnight, I went up to the dock to check on it the next morning. It was still swimming around and trying to get away. Almost absentmindedly, I decided to clean the fish on the dock without first giving it the fridge treatment. I had not foreseen the ordeal of cleaning a live fish (without bashing its head first). I clamped the fish to the cleaning board and started cutting it below the gills in order to slice off a fillet from one side of its body. With the fish thrashing and flopping constantly against the board, it became very difficult for me emotionally and physically to guide the knife smoothly for a clean incision. I botched up my surgery again. I essentially ended up cutting a large slice off the fish including a few ribs.

At the end of this "unkindest cut of all", the fish was still alive, thrashing and squirming as ever. But I soon realized that I had created a horrible scene. I did not know how to kill it and put it out of its misery. I panicked. I threw the fish back in the lake, thinking that it would somehow disappear into the depths of the lake. Instead, it was floating with its partially detached side hanging loose. It was not a pretty sight but at least the fish was dead, I thought. Or, was it?

When a fish floats, is it really dead? It wasn't long before I got the answer. The fish started swimming again. For a moment I got this eerie feeling that the fish was not going to die. Wouldn't it be really terrible if it had to live the rest of its life so badly injured—with one side of its body dangling like that?

After swimming and floating intermittently for a minute or two, the fish finally gave up its ghost—to my great relief. It floated calmly like a fallen leaf on the water with no sign of life. I watched it bob up and down in the water until the waves carried it away—far away out of my sight. But not out of my mind.

The horrific drama of life and death that I had just witnessed made me sick to my stomach. It gave a jolt to my emotions of empathy for the fish. As I was walking back to my house, the gory scenes kept on replaying in my head over and over again. As the time went on, I began to reflect on the ethics of hunting, fishing, and meat-eating. Consequently, I got more and more interested in reading about vegetarianism. I read a book titled *Ethical Vegetarianism: From Pythagoras to Peter Singer.* This book not only provided me a wealth of information about the ethics of vegetarianism, it emotionally transformed me from being thoughtless carnivore to an animal-loving herbivore. While reading a chapter in the book, *The Unpardonable Crime*, I came across the following lines that brought tears in my eyes:

> He looked into the eyes of the beasts and saw there a soul like his own, a soul which could not speak: but the eyes cried for it: 'What have I done to you? Why do you hurt me?'[11]

The above words are from the novel, *Jean-Christophe,* by Romain Rolland (1866–1944), a French novelist and Nobel Laureate in Literature. They are

---

[11] Romain Rolland. The Unpardonable Crime. In: Kerry S. Walters and Lisa Portmess (eds), *Ethical Vegetarianism: From Pythagoras to Peter Singer* (State University of New York, Albany, N.Y., 1999), 137.

spoken by the character Christophe who is haunted by the bloody slaughter of animals at the slaughter house. His words would haunt anyone with a soul. After all, who can watch an animal with trusting eyes being stunned with a crushing blow on the head and then watch it slowly bleed to death? Who can bear to see and hear a cattle bellow or a pig squeal when being dragged to its death chamber? Yet humans, the butchers, go about their job of chopping animal carcasses into pieces without the slightest twinge of empathy in their hearts.

The decision to stop eating meat had a life-changing influence on me. I began to look at animals as fellow creatures sharing the same planet with us. They have the same right to live on earth as we do. They don't have voices to articulate their rights. But we, who have the ability to understand their limitation, have the obligation to protect their unspoken rights.

> There is no fundamental difference between man and the higher mammals in their mental faculties...The difference in mind between man and the higher animals, great as it is, certainly is one of degree and not of kind.[12]

In the above quote Charles Darwin sums up his view of differences in mind between species: It is "one of degree and not of kind." According to Darwin there was continuity in evolution—right from the first single-celled organism to the most complex multi-cellular organism, the modern man.

Evolution bestows universal kinship between all living things. The evolutionary tree of life has grown from a single point of origin and developed many limbs, branches, and leaves over a span of about 3.5 billion years. Animals belong to the same evolutionary tree as humans.

The family tree of animals, including humans, has the same trunk that branched into the animal kingdom about 800 million years ago. Some of the animals grew a notochord (primitive back bone with a dorsal nerve cord) about 550 million years ago, and later some transformed into vertebrates

[12] Charles Darwin, *The Descent of Man and Selection in Relation to Sex*, 2nd Ed. (London: John Murray, 1874), 130.

with spinal columns about 400 million years ago. At this time in evolution, the vertebrate family consisted of a vast variety of animals including fish, amphibians, reptiles, birds, mammals, rodents, and primates.

Some members of the vertebrate family evolved into a class of animals called placental mammals around 100 million years ago. This group included mammals like the cattle, pigs, goats, sheep, deer, camels, horses, whales, and dolphins, to name a few. The same class of animals gave rise to a group called primates around 55 million years ago. The primates included the gorillas, the chimps, and the humans. Homo sapiens or modern humans appeared around 200,000 years ago.

The above short synopsis of evolution provides a glimpse of how humans and food animals evolved from a common stalk. Although the cattle branched out about 95 million years ago, they still carry genes that are not too different from those of humans. Besides similarities of the genetic material, amino acids, proteins, and cell division, they exhibit the same general characteristics of life: reproduction, growth, nutrition, respiration, excretion, senses, and locomotion. Some animals are more similar to us than others but they all share the common thread of life with us.

Most animals that end up at our dinner table are sentient beings, endowed with brains and nervous systems. They are capable of feeling pain, suffering, happiness, and pleasure which can be discerned from their movements, body language, gestures and specific vocal sounds. They lack verbal language but they communicate in many other ways that can be interpreted and understood by a skilled observer. They care for their young just as lovingly and protectively as we do and many in the wild develop social bonds to form families, groups, and communities for mutual well being in a manner that is not too different from humans. Through evolution and natural selection, each species has developed its own strategies to cope with the environment and ensure its survival.

Some people would call animal behavior as nothing more than instinctive. A lot of it appears to be instinctive but it is not that different from humans. All animals are capable of modifying their inherited instincts as a species to best cope with whatever life has dished out for them. They surely learn from experience, although the learning ability varies between species depending on the sophistication of their brain and the impact of the environment in which they live. All species may not have the same brain power but it is brain nonetheless. It works like a brain and it thinks like a brain.

It is not that the general public is unaware of animal abuse at the factory farms. Also it is not that the people are inherently devoid of empathy towards animals. The apparent lack of concern is rather cultural. Like other carnivores, human meat-eaters focus mainly on chomping at their meat in front of them rather than thinking about the living animal from which it came from. They hear of animal abuse but feel little personal responsibility for what happens at these places. Eating meat does not elicit feelings of guilt in them. Meat is just a food. It tastes the same, no matter how the animal was treated before it was killed.

Those who crave baby back ribs are not concerned about how baby pigs are raised. They are oblivious to a piglet's agony when its tail is chopped off or its teeth pulled out (to prevent the piglets biting each other's tail when living in cooped up pens). They have not seen or heard of piglets' tail-cutting or some of them dying of shock because no pain medication is used in these operations. Pork and bacon lovers cannot comprehend the misery of breeding sows when they are confined during pregnancy in gestation crates so tiny that there is not enough room for them to turn around.

Lovers of Kentucky fried chickens never have had the time to think or reflect on de-beaking of live chickens (to prevent vicious fighting or even cannibalism when thousands of these birds are packed into large sheds with very little room to move around). The size of their living space is not larger than half a square foot per bird. Artificial lights are used to prevent the birds from sleeping (rationale being that the sleeping birds don't eat and therefore wouldn't grow as fast as possible). The sleep-deprived birds invariably develop leg problems and many of them die of stressful living.

Beef lovers don't take the time to contemplate on how beef cattle are raised when they look at their neatly trimmed sirloins, tenderloins, or ribeye steaks. They are unmindful of the unsanitary feedlots, where cattle constantly breathe filthy air full of dust and dried manure, often leading to pneumonia and other respiratory illnesses. Many cattle die of feedlot bloat and some develop liver diseases. Antibiotics are routinely added to diets to keep the animal alive until their slaughter. Consumers of meat don't pay attention to the suffering of these animals. Most are unaware of the medications they are ingesting with their meat. There is a complete disconnect in their mind between the meat they eat and the misery of the animal from whose body it was taken.

Hunting of animals for food is ethically at the same level as eating meat. But hunting for pleasure goes a lot further. It is sadistic as well as cowardly. I call it sadistic because enjoyment is being sought through inflicting pain on a sentient being. It is cowardly because animals are defenseless against the weapons and tactics used by the hunters. Baiting, trapping, camouflaging, and other similar tactics cannot be characterized by anything other than cowardly acts of killing through deception. Some hunting fans have even suggested drones for hunting. Poor animals are no match against the human killing machines.

Why do hunters get a kick out of killing wild animals? One reason is the culturally ingrained prejudice whereby animals are considered "subhuman" and, therefore, killing them for food or entertainment is not a moral problem. This widespread prejudice ignores or denies natural kinship between humans and non-humans. It denigrates non-human animals to a stature of inferior life forms. Even some religions maintain the view that humans are special beings – not having evolved from animals. According to some scriptures, humans are created superior to other animals and, thereby, have "dominion" over them. In other words, animals are entirely at the disposal of humans. Because of this deep-rooted cultural and religious bigotry, hunters have lost their natural empathy towards animals. Pictures of hunters smiling and posing with their victims tell it all.

In order to disguise their blatant cruelty, hunters often use language that camouflages the agony and death of their prey. They hide the violence of their hunting pursuit by calling it "game," "sport," or "recreation." They talk about their hunting yield as "harvest," "bag," or "trophies." Some insulate themselves from their killing activity by calling it "wildlife management." It is amazing that this kind of deceptive language goes unchallenged by the general public and is propagated unabashedly by the media through newspapers, TV programs, and magazines. It is a shame that most of the non-hunting public is not perturbed by this deliberate sanitization and glorification of hunting and fishing for fun.

Hunters often claim that they care about wild animals and that they are the "true" conservationists. In their minds, hunting is necessary to keep the animal population under control. But what they miserably fail to conceal is their true passion—the joy of shooting down a wild animal. They say they love nature and wildlife. But what they really love is the killing part of it. If they loved animals, then they would not "kill the thing they love."

Another class of hunting that may look benign on the surface but it is not. It is the "catch and release" type of sport fishing. Catching a fish and then releasing it might seem humane to many, but plunging a hook into its mouth and pulling and tugging it hard while it is struggling for its dear life, is no less painful and terrifying to the fish. One should also be mindful of the fact that a large percentage of the caught and released fish die within a few days. Some may argue that this type of fishing is humane because, in the end, the fish has a chance to live. Yes, but what about the catching part? It is downright torture for the fish. And torture is certainly not humaneness.

Mark Twain (1835 – 1910), an American author and humorist, called man the "Cruel Animal." He said:

> Of all the animals, man is the only one that is cruel. He is the only one that inflicts pain for the pleasure of doing it ... It is a trait that is not known to the higher animals.[13]

I can justify the actions of early man who hunted animals for food, fur, and other necessities of life. What I cannot justify is the modern man's obsession for sport hunting. Deriving pleasure out of taking an innocent life is immoral from anybody's definition of morality. Plain and simple, it is sadistic to get any kind of satisfaction from the suffering and death of an animal. After all the animals are creatures just like us. They feel the pain just like we do. They have the right to live just like us. They belong to the animal kingdom just like us. They are our kin.

In my family, only my daughter Sarah and I are vegetarian. My wife is not a vegetarian (yet?) but is supportive of my being one. My other two daughters are not vegetarian either but they are respectful of my vegetarian life style. On my part, I try not to preach vegetarianism to them or others. But once in a while, I do vent out my feelings as I did in this chapter.

---

[13] Mark Twain, Paul Baender, *What is Man: and Other Philosophical Writings* (University of California Press, LTD., 1973), 84.

Chapter 15

Reflections

When I reflect on my childhood in a tiny rural village in Pakistan, many images pop up in my mind such as running around on the dusty streets of Chak 29, playing games with the kids, riding and grazing my water buffalo, having afternoon tea with my family, and many more. I can't help feeling nostalgic about all that. I had a great childhood. Sometimes I also wonder at the odds of this little kid, me, with so simple a beginning, growing up to be a professor who spends most of his time in retirement reflecting on things like the universe or the purpose of human existence. Maybe, a slow start in the marathon of life is not a handicap.

Until my retirement in 2001, I had not given much thought to the meaning of life. I lived it as I experienced it. I did not feel the need of reflecting deeper on life than living it within the norms and expectations of my family and the society. But soon after retirement, I started reflecting seriously on the meaning of life – What is the purpose of existence? What is this all about? And so on and so on.

Science has helped me understand the beginning of our universe, the origin of life, and its evolution. We now know that the universe came into being 13.7 billion years ago, our solar system was formed about 5 billion years ago, and the earliest life on Earth appeared around 3.5 billion years ago.

Although human evolution goes back to the very origin of life on Earth, modern humans appeared about 300,000 years ago. So, in the words of Carl Sagan (1934 – 1996), an American astronomer and cosmologist: "The cosmos is within us. We are made of star-stuff. We are a way for the universe to know itself."[14]

Humans are an integral part of nature. We sit on top of the evolutionary tree of life and are endowed with brains powerful enough to understand nature itself. Science is our tool of inquiry and of understanding the laws of nature. Accordingly, the task of explaining the meaning of life rightfully belongs to science.

Below are some of the fundamental truths I have learned about life. I consider these truths as logical and universal in scope. They are the guiding principles of my life. I would like to share them with you with the hope that you too will be inspired to launch your own quest for truths – truths to which you could anchor your life.

Freedom of Mind

The human mind is a precious gift of life. We have to make sure that it is free and not controlled by extraneous powers or false beliefs. Also, it is the fundamental right of all human beings to live free and think free. I am a big supporter of Article 18 of the Universal Declaration of Human Rights, adopted by the General Assembly of the United Nations on December 10, 1948, which states:

> Everyone has the right to freedom of thought, conscience and religion; this right includes freedom to change his religion or belief, and freedom, either alone or in community with others and in public or private, to manifest his religion or belief in teaching, practice, worship and observance.

[14] https://quotecatalog.com/quote/carl-sagan-the-cosmos-is-w-X7qNQep/ (accessed July 19, 2018).

It has been said that "the truth shall set you free." But for a truth to be revealed as such, one must cast aside prejudices and preconceived untruths. Once you break out of unreasonable beliefs and prejudices, you are intellectually free. The freedom of mind thus attained allows you to think critically and independently – an essential requirement to distinguish between truth and falsehood. Powered by a free mind, you can self-govern your life without being controlled by others. You can be your own leader – a beacon of light to yourself!

Self-awareness

Self-awareness is an affirmation process mediated by the brain at any time to establish recognition of itself and the surroundings. Thoughts, feelings, action plans, and self-awareness are all states of mind brought about through physiological activity of the brain. All mental experiences are the result of interactions among billions of neurons within the brain.

Scientific studies have shown that thoughts, feelings, memory, and self-awareness originate in our brain. The regions of the brain that are responsible for mental activity are collectively called mind. Our brain contains both the hardware and software of our mental activity. Our mind is not infused with a soul or spirit linked to some supernatural power. The mind is nothing but a product of our own brain's activity.

There is no scientific evidence for a separate entity, called "soul," that is associated with human existence. However, if there is a God-given soul, we have no way of knowing it. Like God, the existence of soul cannot be proved or disproved by science. Does that mean God or soul may still exist even though science cannot prove it one way or the other? Yes, if you believe in God without proof. But to a real scientist, an entity or concept that cannot be approached by science, let alone proven, actually doesn't exist. To believe otherwise would be illogical, unnecessary, or redundant.

Religion

All humans have the fundamental right of choosing and following their own spiritual, religious, humanist, or secular paths in life. We must respect the rights of people to hold diverse beliefs if we want others to respect our beliefs. Human beings are responsible for their own actions – good or bad. Our destinies are in our own hands.

Religions are the spiritual heritage of the human race. They provide the social glue that holds people together. To the faithful, they bring hope in times of despair and give purpose to their lives. That being said, it is also true that most religions foster exclusivity, discrimination, and sectarian conflict. Historically, they have caused wars, persecution, and misery for those who did not believe. Literal conformity to the religious scriptures has given rise to fundamentalist movements which do not bode well for either the religions or their believers.

A theocracy or a government that makes laws based on religious doctrine invariably undermines the rights of the religious minorities or the non-believing citizenry. Such governments are undemocratic by definition. A true constitutional democracy, on the other hand, requires majority rule but at the same time guarantees full protection of the minority rights. For that reason, I am a big fan of the First Amendment to the Constitution of the United States which states: "Congress shall make no law respecting an establishment of religion, or prohibiting the free exercise thereof; …."

Morality and Ethics

Morality refers to principles of right and wrong in human conduct. Ethics is the system or code of morals. The two terms are often used interchangeably. Ethics may also be called moral philosophy.

Human conduct or behavior may be characterized as moral or immoral depending on whether or not it conforms to the generally accepted standards of goodness or rightness in conduct or behavior. Moral standards may be based on criteria set collectively by a society, religion, or a particular philosophy. As these criteria change with time, so do the moral standards. It is important for us to understand that as human civilization evolves, morality also evolves to stay relevant to its contemporary needs and moral values. Even though certain moral standards may be relatively constant with time and universally agreed on, their correct application to specific situations at specific times may cause controversy and debate. Resolution of such debates may bring about a revision or reaffirmation of the existing standards of morality.

Should morality be considered relativistic? Are all moral judgments derived from religious sources, cultures, events, or people? Is there an objective morality that could be based on scientific logic? Answers to the above questions are difficult to find because morality is a subject that is not easily amenable to objective analysis. In an article, Eugene Khutoryansky provides a good discussion of these issues and argues that morality can in fact be based on or justified by scientific reasoning. His position is that morality is linked to human emotions such as suffering, fear, compassion, love, hate, envy, and jealousy. By scientifically analyzing human emotions, the basis for objective morality can be found. For example, according to Khutoryansky:

> It is only by experiencing suffering ourselves that we can come to understand what suffering is and the fact that it is wrong to inflict it needlessly. This, however, should not come as a surprise. All science is based on observation.[15]

My favorite of all the principles of morality and ethics is the Golden Rule. The Golden Rule is founded on *empathy*—an innate propensity for feeling the emotions of others. Wikipedia defines empathy as "the capacity to recognize and, to some extent, share feelings (such as sadness or happiness) that are being experienced by another sentient or semi-sentient being."[16]

---

[15] Khutoryansky, Eugene, *Objective Morality Based on Scientific and Rational Reasoning.* http://members.aol.com/okhutor/essay/morals.html (accessed May 27, 2006).

[16] http://en.wikipedia.org/wiki/The_Golden_Rule#Scientific_research (Accessed June 20, 2011)

This inborn trait is woven into the fabric of our moral being. It makes us feel the pain of others and keeps us from treating others in ways that we would not like to be treated. The trait is there unless one deliberately turns it off.

Perspectives on Life

Looking back at my life, I feel like a real-life actor who appears on the stage of life without a script. I learned to act my part from my family, friends, teachers, and the world at large. The play is still continuing but I take a little pause to get a perspective on my life and the human life in general. Below are some of my reflections on life.

I do not subscribe to a particular philosophy or belief system. I feel happy that I have a free mind which allows me to make my own decisions and self-direct my life as best as I can. If I do have to characterize my life philosophy, it would probably be closest to what is called existentialism. From a brief description of this philosophy below, you would know why I like its basic tenets. Most importantly for me, it embodies freedom of mind.

Existentialism, as defined by Google dictionary, is "a philosophical theory or approach that emphasizes the existence of the individual person as a free and responsible agent determining their own development through acts of the will." Jean-Paul Sartre (1905 – 1980), a French philosopher, maintained that humans exist first before they change their essence or nature as individuals. In other words, humans make themselves what they are by making choices based on their experience and interactions with the world into which they have been thrust. In Sartre's words:

> What is meant here by saying that existence precedes essence? It means first of all, man exists, turns up, appears on the scene, and, only afterwards, defines himself.[17]

[17] https://www.goodreads.com/work/quotes/2376452-l-existentialisme-est-un-humanisme] (Accessed April 16, 2018).

Human Condition

When humans first roamed the earth, life was not easy. In the words of an American anthropologist, William Howells (1908 – 2005):

> Man's life is hard, very hard. And he knows it, poor soul; that is the thing. He knows that he is forever confronted with the Four Horsemen – death, famine, disease, and the malice of other men.[18]

Although modern man is still confronted with the Four Horsemen, the pattern of the human condition has become more varied and complex. Human life is still not a bed of roses, but it is not a bed of nails either. For some who are lucky to be born in affluence, their life is expected to be comfortable unless something unforeseen wrecks it or they screw it up on their own. For others who are less fortunate, life has a built-in handicap but it can still be turned around into a joyful experience. The poor just have to work at it harder or be luckier.

Another view of life worth mentioning is that of existential nihilism. According to this view, life has no intrinsic meaning or value. Humans are thrust into existence without knowing "why." It is only through necessity or illusion that they create their own subjective meaning of life and purpose. This idea sounds somewhat similar to what William Shakespeare says in *Macbeth* [Act V, scene 5, line 23]:

> Life's but a walking shadow, a poor player,
> That struts and frets his hour upon the stage,
> And then is heard no more. It is a tale
> Told by an idiot, full of sound and fury,
> Signifying nothing.

And yet, for some, including me, it doesn't matter whether you are rich or poor or whether life has some inherent meaning or purpose. Life is just great as it is. It reminds me of the song by Louis Armstrong (1901 – 1971):

---

[18] W. W. Howells, *The Heathens* (Garden City, N. Y: Doubleday, 1948).

I see trees of green, red roses too
I see them bloom for me and you
And I think to myself what a wonderful world

Epilogue

Since I left Pakistan for America in 1963, my parents and all of my siblings have passed away. I conclude my memoir with their names and their loving memories.

Father: Mohammad Nawaz Khan (Pathan Niazi Wada Isakhel)
Mother: Ayesha-Fatima Bibi (daughter of Azeem Khan Pathan Niazi Wada Isakhel)
Sisters: Sardaran Bibi, Meeran Bibi, and Alam Khatoon
Brothers: Rab Nawaz, Haq Nawaz, Shah Nawaz, Zulfiqar Ali, Abul Satar, and Dost Mohammad

Faiz M. Khan

About the Author

Faiz M. Khan was a Fulbright scholar and received his doctorate degree in Biophysics from the University of Minnesota. He joined the University of Minnesota as faculty in 1968 and became full professor in 1979. He retired as professor emeritus in 2001. He has published eleven books and over eighty research articles.

Printed in the United States
By Bookmasters